Lydia Maria Child

The Quest for Racial Justice

OXFORD
PORTRAITS

Lydia Maria Child

The Quest for Racial Justice

Lori Kenschaft

OXFORD
UNIVERSITY PRESS

OXFORD
UNIVERSITY PRESS

Oxford New York
Auckland Bangkok Buenos Aires Cape Town Chennai
Dar es Salaam Delhi Florence Hong Kong Istanbul Karachi Kolkata
Kuala Lumpur Madrid Melbourne Mexico City Mumbai Nairobi
São Paulo Shanghai Singapore Taipei Tokyo Toronto

and an associated company in
Berlin

Published by Oxford University Press, Inc.
198 Madison Avenue, New York, New York 10016
www.oup.com

Oxford is a registered trademark of Oxford University Press

Design: Greg Wozney
Layout: Alexis Siroc
Picture Research: Jennifer Smith

Library of Congress Cataloging-in-Publication Data
Kenschaft, Lori
Lydia Maria Child / Lori Kenschaft.
p. cm.–(Oxford portraits)
Includes bibliographical references and index.
Summary: A biography of a popular writer who, in the mid-19th century, gave
up her literary success to fight for the abolition of slavery, for women's rights, and
for the fair treatment of American Indians.
ISBN: 0-19-513257-2
1. Child, Lydia Maria Francis, 1802–1880—Juvenile literature. 2. Women social
reformers—Unites States—Biography—Juvenile literature. 3. Women abolitionists
—United States—Biography—Juvenile literature. 4. Authors, American—
19th century—Biography—Juvenile literature. [1. Child, Lydia Maria Francis,
1802–1888. 2. Authors, American. 3. Abolitionists. 4. Women—Biography.]
I. Title. II. Oxford Portraits Series.
HQ1413.C45 K46 2002
303.48'4'092-dc21
[B]   2001052339

9 8 7 6 5 4 3 2 1

Printed in the United States of America on acid-free paper

On the cover: Lydia Maria Child in 1865, the year the Civil War ended
Frontispiece: Lydia Maria Francis in 1826, the year she started publishing the
Juvenile Miscellany

CONTENTS

1

THE LOVE OF BOOKS

Lydia Maria Child was a popular young author in 1833 when she published her *Appeal in Favor of That Class of Americans Called Africans,* which described the horrors of slavery. Her appeal called for immediate emancipation of all slaves and urged Americans to turn their vague antislavery feelings into an organized abolitionist movement. Within weeks, public outrage had destroyed her career. Many people canceled their subscriptions to a magazine she edited, refused to buy her other books, or snubbed her on the street. Old friends no longer allowed her in their homes. Her literary mentor, the influential Harvard professor George Ticknor, not only refused to see her himself but also refused to associate with anyone who was seen talking with her.

These friends were soon replaced, however, by new ones who were drawn to abolitionism by Child's arguments. Charles Sumner, the future senator and congressional leader of the abolitionist cause, always credited the *Appeal* with awakening him to the injustice of slavery. So did Wendell Phillips, who was to become one of the greatest orators of the abolitionist movement. Throughout her life, Child would meet men and women from all walks of life who would thank her for stirring their consciences and making them see that—no matter how modest or exalted their position—they had some power to help eradicate slavery.

Within months, Child was an acknowledged leader of the abolitionist movement. Only William Lloyd Garrison, the fiery evangelical Christian preacher who had already made the abolition of slavery his life's goal, had more stature and influence. Child's approach was more calm and rational than Garrison's. Slavery, she argued, hurts everyone—even slaveholders, who must endure the inefficiencies of coerced labor and risk dying in a slave insurrection. Abolition is therefore not just the most moral choice but also the most practical one. Child's detailed arguments, well supported by historical research, reached many people who were turned off by Garrison's passionate rhetoric.

It was dangerous to be an abolitionist in the 1830s. Two months after Child published her *Appeal*, mob violence against abolitionists broke out across the country. In the North, crowds of angry men set fire to homes, offices, and meeting halls, destroying many public buildings and several black neighborhoods. They also demolished abolitionist printing presses, attacked those attending abolitionist meetings with brickbats and rotten eggs, and threatened to lynch abolitionist leaders. In 1837 Elijah Lovejoy, the editor of an antislavery newspaper in Alton, Illinois, was killed when he tried to protect his printing press from a mob. In the South, indignant defenders of tradition hanged abolitionist leaders in effigy, and no one had much doubt that they would do so for real if they could. Abolitionists therefore stayed out of the South and sent antislavery newspapers and pamphlets instead. When the first pamphlets arrived, mobs broke into post offices, ransacked them for antislavery publications, and burned whatever they found in great bonfires.

Official responses to the antislavery movement were no more encouraging. In 1836 the U.S. Congress passed a "gag rule," which decreed that any petition or resolution regarding

The crowd used all sorts of weapons to destroy Elijah Lovejoy's Illinois office and printing press in November 1837. Many abolitionist leaders suffered similar attacks, and Lovejoy himself had survived the demolition of three previous presses. This time, however, he was killed.

slavery would be immediately and permanently tabled without discussion. After the post office riots, the postmaster general declared that any local postmaster could, if he chose, refuse to deliver abolitionist literature. It would be another 30 years before slaves would have their freedom—and in the 1830s it looked like it might be a lot longer than that.

Throughout those years Child tried to balance her work for social justice, her love of literature, and her need to make a living. She became an advocate for Indians as well as slaves, and eventually an advocate for women's rights as well. Unlike many abolitionists, she believed that racial prejudice in the North was almost as bad as slavery in the South. Racial discrimination of any form, she constantly insisted, should have no place in a republic based on the ideals of equality, freedom, and opportunity. After the slaves were freed she tried—unsuccessfully—to ensure that they would become fully equal members of American society.

Child was always poor, and she never regained the popularity as a writer that she had enjoyed before she published the *Appeal*. She did, however, manage to support herself with her pen and have some money left over to give to the causes she believed in. She was an innovative and successful journalist and published a total of 52 books, including novels, histories, collections of short stories, biographies, and, of course, many polemical works arguing for abolition and racial justice. She was often discouraged, but she never gave up on her dream of a society in which people would not be divided by race.

The American Revolution was still a recent memory when Lydia was born on February 11, 1802. Both of her parents had been nine years old when the Revolution began. Her mother, Susannah Rand, lived with her family on Bunker Hill in Charlestown, Massachusetts. Almost the entire town burned to the ground when the British captured Bunker Hill in 1775. The family fled with whatever they could carry and lost everything else. Lydia's father, Convers Francis, came from a family of Patriots. His father fought in the Battle of Lexington and promptly enlisted in the revolutionary army, while his mother did the best she could to feed her 10 children by herself. There were not many ways for a woman to make money in those days, and one winter the family almost starved. Finally, a neighbor gave them a barrel of potatoes that allowed them to survive until spring.

When Convers and Susannah married, they were determined that their children would not suffer as they had. Convers became a successful

A kneeling slave pleads for her freedom in the frontispiece to Lydia Maria Child's An Appeal in Favor of That Class of Americans Called Africans. *Its publication in 1833 thrust Child to the forefront of the abolitionist movement.*

baker in Medford, Massachusetts. His biscuits—known as Medford crackers—were sold not just in Medford and Boston, but even in England. Susannah was a hardworking housewife. At that time there were no factories for making clothing, no stores where you could pick up food for dinner. Women like Susannah made clothes at home, gardened and traded for food in the summer, and preserved everything the family would eat for the winter. A housewife's skills determined how well her family would be clothed and fed.

Susannah and Convers quickly had four children: James, Susannah, Mary, and Convers, Jr. Then, after a gap of six years, they had another baby, whom they named Lydia. They had apparently hoped not to have any more children, and Lydia always felt that she was unwanted and unloved. Her father spent all his time in the bakery, where girls were not welcome. Her mother was always busy and sick and had little interest in her youngest child. By this time the family was reasonably well-off, so Lydia was never cold and hungry the way her parents had been, but she had few happy memories of her childhood.

Fortunately, Convers, Jr., was very fond of his little sister. He loved to read, and in Lydia's earliest memories he always had his nose in some book. Lydia started borrowing his books as soon as she learned to read, and by the time she was 10 she was reading Shakespeare. She did not understand everything she read, of course, but Convers was always willing to answer her questions.

Lydia's parents were practical people, and they did not approve of this love of books. They expected their daughter to be a housewife and Convers to be an artisan like his father—a baker probably, or some other kind of small proprietor who worked with his hands. In either case, they felt, book-learning was poor preparation for the responsibilities of adult life. At the time, most children went to school for only a few years, and they were expected to learn only to read and write and do arithmetic. This knowledge was practical. Any good Protestant had to be able to read the Bible, and being able to write and do sums was useful for a shopkeeper or housewife. Beyond that, many people felt that education was not just a waste of time but might also make children discontented with their lot in life.

Convers wanted to go to college, but his father refused to consider the idea. However, Dr. John Brooks—then the family physician and later the governor of Massachusetts—told him that it would be a shame to waste Convers's exceptional intellectual abilities. Many years later, Lydia remembered Brooks's argument: "He has remarkable powers of mind; and his passion for books is so strong that he will be sure to distinguish himself in learning; whereas, if you

Lydia's older brother, Convers Francis, became a well-respected minister in Watertown, Massachusetts. His ornate chair, expensive clothing, and grim expression all reflect his sense of the dignity appropriate to a clergyman.

try to make anything else of him, he will prove a total failure." Apparently Brooks was convincing, for Convers was sent to the local academy, where every other student came from a rich family, and then to Harvard University. After he graduated, he became a Unitarian minister. With the help of Brooks and several other mentors, he found a way to put his love of book-learning to use.

No one considered sending Lydia to college, of course. For one thing, not a single college in the country would admit girls, and it would be another 30 years before the first coeducational college would open its doors. For another thing, everyone agreed that higher education was useless for a girl, and might make her unhappy with her duties as a wife and mother. Lydia was no less intellectually talented than Convers, and her passion for books was as great, but she received only a fragmented education. She spent a year or so in each of four different schools, where she learned to read and then was introduced to French, music, and other accomplishments considered appropriate for young ladies. Almost everything she learned, however, she taught herself with the help of her brother.

Lydia was nine when Convers left home to go to Harvard, and she felt lonely and miserable after he was gone. All of a sudden she was without her constant companion, her teacher, the person she loved most in the world. Her favorite sister, Susannah, married and left the home that same year, adding to Lydia's loneliness. Her mother had been sick for several years, and now she became a bedridden invalid. James had already left home, and their father was busy in the bakery, so only Mary was left to take care of the household and their sick mother. Lydia spent most of her time alone.

Three years later, after a long, lingering illness, Susannah finally died. Lydia had grown used to seeing her mother so sick and weak and was no longer afraid of losing her. One day when Lydia was in a bad mood, her mother asked her to fetch a glass of water and Lydia tried to refuse the request. When Susannah insisted, Lydia brought the water but set it down quickly and left the room without a word. Susannah died later that afternoon, and Lydia felt overwhelmed by guilt and regret as well as grief. For the rest of her life, she wished that she had responded more generously to her mother's last request.

Convers, Sr., became very grim and forbidding after his wife's death. As a devout Calvinist Christian with harsh views, he believed that life is a place of suffering, that God had decreed that most people would be damned, and that there was nothing an individual could do to increase his or her chance of salvation. He feared that Susannah had entered the everlasting torments of hell and suspected that he would eventually join her there. Gloomy by nature, he had always tended to be curt and gruff. Now he devoted himself to his work and had few words to spare for his daughter.

Lydia's losses continued. In August her grandmother died, and the following March her favorite sister, Susannah, died. In between, Mary got married and moved to Maine. Lydia refused to attend the ceremony. She had no desire to celebrate the departure of her last remaining sibling.

Lydia and her father were now alone in the house. Her father was silent and uncommunicative, and Lydia was soon to turn 13—a tumultuous age for many people. Convers disapproved of his daughter's interest in literature and tried to discourage her from reading. He believed she should study the practical, feminine arts of cooking and sewing, not fill her mind with useless stories. Lydia continued to read whatever she could get her hands on, but she was restless and unhappy. Although her father meant well, he had no idea how to guide a teenage daughter—especially one with intellectual inclinations.

After a year of this uncomfortable arrangement, Convers decided to send Lydia to live with her sister Mary in Norridgewock, Maine. Mary was now expecting her first baby, and Lydia's help with housework and child care was very welcome. Norridgewock was on the Kennebec River, 20 miles north of Augusta, and much of the year it was cut off from the outside world by ice and snow. Life there was much like it had been in Massachusetts a hundred years earlier. Women cooked over open fireplaces, spun their own thread and wove their own cloth, and made their own soap and candles. In the winter the snow might come up to a second-floor window, and the summers—when all the food for the year had to be grown, gathered, or slaughtered—were short. One summer it snowed in June, and frosts in July and August killed all the corn.

Lydia spent much of her time learning how to survive in a frontier settlement. With a growing household, there was always clothing to make and food to prepare or preserve for the winter. In her little bits of free time, Child attended the local school, which was open to boys in the winter and girls in the summer, and corresponded with her brother Convers, who encouraged her to keep reading. Norridgewock's library was small but unusually good for a frontier town, and Lydia was one of its most frequent visitors. She especially enjoyed Shakespeare and Milton and the historical romances of Sir Walter Scott, which portrayed vibrant characters in distant times and places.

Mary's husband, Warren Preston, was a young and ambitious lawyer who soon became a leading citizen of Norridgewock. He was one of a new breed of settler: rebellious against New England's religious, political, and cultural traditions, he wanted to create a community where he could live as he pleased. He rejected, for example, the traditional Calvinism that was so important to Lydia's father, and helped found the religiously liberal Norridgewock Unitarian Society, which had a more optimistic view of human nature and of the potential for human happiness both in this life and the next.

When Lydia arrived in Norridgewock in 1815, Maine was still part of Massachusetts but a separationist movement was growing. During the recent War of 1812 several towns in Maine had been occupied by British troops, and the state government in Boston had made no attempt to come to their aid. Men like Warren Preston already resented Boston's political and cultural power, and they argued that Maine would be better off on its own. In December 1819 the people of Maine overwhelmingly voted to adopt a new state constitution. All they needed was the approval of Congress to become an independent state.

Normally, Congress would approve such requests without debate, but this was not a normal time. Missouri had also recently applied to become a state. In 1787 Congress had banned slavery north of the Ohio River but had not decided whether slavery would be allowed west of the Mississippi River. Now Missouri—which was north of where the Ohio met the Mississippi—wanted to enter the Union as a slave state.

Most Northerners opposed the expansion of slavery into new areas. They considered slavery "non-republican": an unfortunate exception to the American principles of liberty and equality. They argued that although the Constitution allowed the Southern states to keep their slaves, the Founding Fathers intended to limit slavery to where it already existed. If slavery were allowed in the new states, free settlers would not be able to compete with the slave-powered plantations on an equal basis, and the country would gradually move ever more toward slavery. Southerners, however, feared that the slave system would be doomed if it were not allowed to expand. Plantation agriculture was very hard on the soil, and after a few generations planters had to move on to fresh land. If they could not take their slaves with them, they would lose all the money they had invested in them. Both Southerners and Northerners also feared that admitting new states would

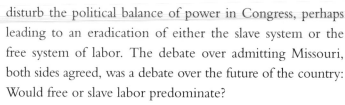

disturb the political balance of power in Congress, perhaps leading to an eradication of either the slave system or the free system of labor. The debate over admitting Missouri, both sides agreed, was a debate over the future of the country: Would free or slave labor predominate?

After a long stalemate, the Speaker of the House, Henry Clay, finally brokered a compromise. Missouri would be admitted as a slave state and Maine would be admitted as a free state, thereby preserving the balance in Congress. Many people in Maine objected to this compromise, which they saw as a capitulation to the Southerners. Others, however, argued that if Maine did not accept the compromise, it might never become a state. Practicality won, and Maine entered the Union in 1820. Living in Warren Preston's household, Lydia heard all these arguments and got her first introduction to real-world politics.

Lydia felt an obligation to disprove the common stereotypes of Indians as violent and exotic, which were conveyed by pictures such as this one of the Reverend Peter Jones wielding an ax and dressed in a mish-mash of Indian garb.

More important at the time, however, was her contact with Native Americans. Norridgewock got its name from an Abenaki group that had formerly lived in the area. They had been massacred in 1724 by British troops, who also killed a Jesuit priest who lived in the village and destroyed the Catholic church he had built. British settlers then took over the land. Just a few months after Lydia arrived, a great storm overturned a large oak tree and revealed the old church bell, which had been buried in the ground for almost a century. This surprising event formed the basis of two of Lydia's earliest published stories—"Adventures of a Bell" and "The Church in the Wilderness."

Abenaki and Penobscot Indians still lived near Norridgewock, and Lydia often visited their villages or met them in their travels. She enjoyed listening to the stories the women told as they prepared food or wove and dyed their baskets. She would usually take gifts when she went to visit them because the Indians had been driven off all the best lands and were now very poor. One especially snowy winter an Indian woman showed up at the door and asked for salt fish, explaining that the snow made it impossible for her to get food. The next day she returned with her baby, who had been born in the meantime. According to her tribe's custom, she told the amazed white people, she had washed the newborn in the river—after chopping a hole in the ice with a hatchet. This time she asked for a sack of potatoes, which she slung over her shoulder and carried four miles to her village, with the baby, through the deep snow.

Lydia always remembered the physical strength of Native American women. Many 19th-century Americans believed that women were frail and weak by nature, but Lydia knew that women could be hearty and vigorous. If women are weak, she argued throughout her life, it is because of their deficient education and poor habits, not their biology. She herself was always physically active, and she remained strong and healthy well past her 70th birthday.

The years in Norridgewock were good for Lydia. She found good spirits, good health, and good friends. She had never been happier, she wrote to her brother Convers shortly after her 18th birthday. In the same letter she told him that she had agreed to be a teacher in Gardiner, 40 miles away. She was afraid she might be lonely in Gardiner, she confessed, but she looked forward to being independent. She was happy and confident and ready to explore the world.

Lydia hoped this frontispiece to her book, First Settlers of New England *(1828), would demonstrate Indians' sympathy with a peaceful and abundant natural landscape. She intended to impress young people with their duty to "allevi-ate, as much as is in their power, the suffer-ings of the generous and interesting race of men whom we have so unjustly supplanted."*

The teaching job was apparently not all she had hoped, however, for a year later she accepted Convers's offer to live with him. He had just become the minister of the Unitarian church in Watertown, Massachusetts, and had a big parson-age with many empty rooms—and an excellent library. One of Lydia's first actions after she returned to Massachusetts was to get herself rebaptized Lydia Maria and ask all her family and friends to call her Maria. The name Lydia, she later explained in a letter, had "some associations of child-hood" that were "unpleasant" to her. She had returned to the geographic area of her childhood, but she did not want to return to her childhood feelings.

For the next few years Maria read avidly in her brother's library, where she finally got a solid grounding in history and philosophy and classical literature. She also met Convers's friends, several of whom were among the greatest intellectuals of the day. Ralph Waldo Emerson, for example, was then a student at Harvard, and Maria would watch his growing career with great interest. Most important, she developed a new ambition of her own. She wanted not only to read books, but to write them too.

2

A RISING STAR

One lazy Sunday afternoon in 1824, Maria was sitting in her brother's library and leafing through old magazines. She happened to come across a review of a long poem, titled *Yamoyden,* that told the story of King Philip's War, the longest, bloodiest, and most history-shaping of the wars between Native Americans and colonists in the 17th century. Maria knew the author of the review, Convers's friend John Gorham Palfrey, so she read it with extra interest.

The first great American writer, Palfrey predicted, would be one who, like the authors of *Yamoyden,* drew on the native dramas of America—its Puritans and Indians and unparalleled natural beauty. The United States was still a young country in the 1820s, and many people wondered whether its experiment in republican government would succeed. As the revolutionary generation died, some feared that Americans might revert to the aristocratic habits of their European ancestors and look to a monarch for leadership. Literary patriots like Palfrey therefore considered it important to create a distinctively American culture: one rooted in the New World that would reduce the power of European history to shape Americans' imaginations.

The sources of this new culture were not obvious. Americans habitually looked to Europe and patterned themselves on its ways. To a large degree, they ate European foods, read European books, and admired European art and architecture. They had also, however, been exposed to Native American cultures. They had learned to eat Indian foods, such as corn, and some Americans realized that these tribes had complex storytelling traditions that were comparable to European writings. Palfrey suggested that the interweaving of European and Indian themes could lead to a distinctively American literature—one that would allow Americans to see themselves not just as Europeans overseas, but as a new and different people.

According to Maria's later account, she was so inspired by Palfrey's ideas that she immediately picked up a pen and started to write. By the time she was called to afternoon services, she had finished the first chapter of what would become her first book, *Hobomok, a Tale of Early Times.* Her brother Convers was enormously impressed by the quality of her work. "But Maria did you *really* write this?" she later recalled him asking. With his enthusiastic encouragement she finished the novel in six weeks.

Hobomok tells the story of a young Puritan woman, Mary Conant, who is drawn to two possible husbands: the Englishman Charles Brown (who, as an Episcopalian, is unacceptable to her devout Puritan father) and the Indian Hobomok (who is, of course, no more acceptable). After Mary hears that Charles has drowned in a shipwreck, she marries Hobomok and has a child with him. Charles eventually returns, however, and Hobomok decides that Mary and their child belong with Charles. Hobomok disappears into the woods, never to return.

This book's positive images of Indian culture and intermarriage were both unusual and controversial. Most 19th-century writings about contacts between Indians and whites implied that they could never understand each other, that war between the two groups was inevitable, and that Indians were doomed to extinction. Maria, however, suggested the alternative of intermarriage and cultural assimilation. Ultimately, she still imagined Native American cultures as disappearing— but through the gradual process of cultural change rather than through bloodshed and genocide.

Like most authors in the 1820s, Maria had to pay for her book to be published and had to publicize it herself. She borrowed $495 (presumably from her father or brother) and paid to have a thousand copies printed, which were offered for sale at 75¢ each. Unfortunately, not many of them sold. The influential *North American Review* declared that her plot—with its interracial love affair and happy remarriage

In the mid-1800s, images of interracial couples continued to be shocking. The actress Lola Montez had her daguerreotype taken with a Cheyenne man, Alights on a Cloud, when he was part of a political delegation to Washington in the 1850s.

after an amicable divorce—was "revolting." Maria could not pay back her debt, and it looked like her budding literary career was over.

Then Maria heard that Harvard professor of literature George Ticknor had spoken well of *Hobomok*. Ticknor was so influential in New England literary circles that his opinion could make or break any young writer. Maria audaciously decided to write to him. Since he had already "voluntarily praised my trifling production," she asked, would he be willing to exert his "influence in the literary and fashionable world" on behalf of her "unfortunate book"?

Ticknor responded with enthusiasm. He arranged for a longer and more positive review to be published in the *North American Review*. He invited Maria to social events at his home and around Boston. He even offered to pay off her remaining debt for the book's publication—but that was no longer necessary because the book had started to sell well.

As Ticknor's protégée, Maria was soon celebrated as a rising young author and invited to the most fashionable parties. The baker's daughter was welcomed into Boston's best homes, where parlors were filled with Persian carpets and crystal chandeliers and silk wall hangings imported from China. She received many tokens of her new friends' esteem— books, jewelry, pictures, and invitations to elaborate dinner parties, where she might well be one of the guests of honor. She often felt that her straightforward manners and plain clothing were out of place in her elegant surroundings, but she also enjoyed the attention. She became, she later confessed, "a 'little wee bit' of a lion." In 1825 the governor of Massachusetts, Levi Lincoln, invited her to a reception to meet General Lafayette, the French hero of the American Revolution. Maria always felt that one of the high points of her life occurred when the general kissed her hand.

Even with her new popularity, however, Maria did not have enough income to pay for her food and clothing. She disliked being dependent on her brother, so she set to work

Many people of Maria's generation felt that General Lafayette was as much or more of a hero than George Washington. Maria linked the two heroes in her History of the Condition of Women, *which showed Washington's mother greeting Lafayette in her garden.*

on her second and third books. *Evenings in New England* was a collection of children's stories published just in time for the 1824 Christmas gift-giving season. Her second historical novel, *The Rebels,* appeared in 1825. Set in revolutionary-era Boston, it emphasized women's contributions to the creation of the young country. Many years later Maria was amused to discover that a speech she wrote for the revolutionary leader James Otis seemed so realistic that it was reprinted in many schoolbooks as an actual, authentic speech. Generations of 19th-century children memorized her words, thinking they were those of Otis.

Maria was always looking for new projects and a more reliable source of income, so she was interested when a Boston publisher invited her to edit a children's magazine modeled on *Evenings in New England.* The first issue of the

Juvenile Miscellany appeared in September 1826, and its sub-scription list grew almost daily. Within four months it had 850 subscribers. This was the country's first successful chil-dren's magazine, and Maria took great pleasure in thinking of the many children who read each issue—and of her now-ample income of $300 a year.

In the early 19th century, people were only just begin-ning to think of writing for children as different from writ-ing for adults. In previous generations, children were con-sidered to be small adults: they did the same work as adults as soon as they physically could, and they learned to read by studying the Bible and perhaps also Milton, Shakespeare, and sermons. During the 19th century, however, people began to think of childhood as a precious stage of life that was important for future development. One result was that adults began to feel that children needed books of their own—books that would give them moral instruction and help them grow up to be loyal and virtuous members of the American republic. Much of the new writing for children was intensely religious and preachy. Writers for children delighted in stories of religious conversion, heart-wrench-ing deathbed scenes and angelic children who could do no wrong.

Children, however, tended to prefer Maria's writing. They often shared issues of the *Miscellany* and eagerly looked forward to its arrival. "The children sat on the stone steps of their house doors all the way up and down Chestnut Street in Boston, waiting for the [mail] carrier," one of her young readers later remembered. "The fortunate possessor of the first copy found a crowd of little ones hanging over her shoulder from the steps above. . . . How forlorn we were if the carrier were late!" Maria's stories often had moral lessons, but they also reflected her cheerful sense of humor and wide-ranging curiosity. Every issue of the *Miscellany* contained not only short stories (often set in exotic parts of the world or in old New England) but also puzzles and riddles, essays on history and science, poems, and engraved illustrations. Maria often told stories of children who found success and happiness through the virtues of hard work, frugality, loyalty, and perseverance, but her stories were never boring.

Not surprisingly, this successful and vivacious young writer attracted the admiration of young men as well as children. Maria was short, with dark hair and dark eyes, and her features were not considered beautiful by the standards of her time. She was also intelligent and witty, enthusiastic and self-educated, and passionate in her convictions. Young ladies were supposed to be gentle and submissive, and many people felt that Maria was too inclined to speak her mind. Some, however, found her qualities enormously attractive. Among them were the artist Francis Alexander, who convinced Maria to let him paint her portrait, and the young writer Nathaniel Parker Willis.

Maria, however, was not at all sure that she wanted to marry. She enjoyed her work as a writer and editor, and she appreciated the freedom that financial independence gave her. She had watched her mother and sister, and now Convers's wife, Abby, struggle with the demands of motherhood at a time when many women had five or six children or more. The success of the *Miscellany* made it possible for her to imagine a life of literary independence. She preferred money to fame, she wrote to her sister Mary, especially because she had a "reasonable prospect of being always single."

One man complicated this prospect. Maria had met David Lee Child in 1824, when he was a newcomer to Watertown and Convers invited him to dinner. Like Maria, David came from a modest background. He was one of 12 children of a poor farmer in West Boylston, Massachusetts, and had spent much of his childhood toting water and doing other farm chores. But he also had great intellectual gifts, and despite his family's poverty he had found his way to Harvard. He was fluent in French, German, Spanish, Portuguese, Latin, and Greek, enormously knowledgeable

THE

JUVENILE MISCELLANY.

THIRD SERIES. VOL. 3.

With what delight he pores
O'er the bright pages of his pictured stores;
How oft he steals upon your graver task,
Of this to tell you, and of that to ask,
And when the waning hour to bedward bids,
Though gentle sleep sit waiting on his lids,
How winningly he pleads to gain you o'er,
That he may read one little story more.

Sprague.

BY MRS. D. L. CHILD,

AUTHOR OF EVENINGS IN N. ENGLAND, THE FRUGAL HOUSE-
WIFE, THE GIRL'S OWN BOOK, THE MOTHER'S BOOK, &C.&C.

The title page of Child's Juvenile Miscellany reflected American society's new emphasis on the importance of careful parenting. The reality was that most families still struggled to meet their children's basic needs for food and clothing.

about politics, and had recently returned from two years in Europe.

David originally went to Portugal as a diplomatic attaché. Nine months later France invaded Spain in order to defend the Spanish king against revolutionaries who wanted to establish a constitutional form of government. David saw the Spanish revolution as similar to the American Revolution, and he abandoned his post in order to join the revolutionary army and support the cause of liberty. Within a few months, however, the rebellion had failed and David was dismissed from his diplomatic position. He returned to the United States and, not sure what to do next, went to Watertown to study law with his uncle.

Maria found David supremely romantic. He was brilliant in his conversation, uncompromising in his defense of freedom, and marvelously articulate in expressing his views. He had the education and knowledge of the world that Maria had long desired, and he made no secret of his admiration for the intelligent young author. His good looks—dark hair, high forehead, and passionate eyes—added to his charm. Child wrote in her diary: "He is the most gallant man that has lived since the sixteenth century; and needs nothing but helmet, shield, and chain armour to make him a complete knight of chivalry."

In many ways, however, David did not look like a good prospect for a husband. At the age of 31, he still did not have an established profession, frequently asked his impoverished parents for money, and had acquired a substantial amount of debt during his travels. He repeatedly embraced idealistic causes without thinking about their consequences and was often deceived by his overly positive responses to charismatic figures. If he believed someone was right, he would follow their lead no matter what the cost.

There were signs, however, that David's prospects might be improving. He was the editor of the *Massachusetts Journal,* a political newspaper that was much favored by the President of the United States, John Quincy Adams, and by one of the country's most influential senators, Daniel Webster. Webster considered David a protégé, and Governor Lincoln of Massachusetts also thought highly of him. Within a few years David would be elected to the Massachusetts state legislature, at which point it seemed as if he might be headed toward a successful career as a lawyer and politician.

Although they were intensely attracted to each other, Maria was reluctant to give up her independence, and David was reluctant to ask her to marry him until his future was more secure. For three years they talked and argued. David continued to be fascinated by this intelligent, articulate, opinionated, and forceful woman, while Maria continued to enjoy intense conversations with a man who truly treated her as his equal.

Finally, in October 1827, David asked Maria to marry him. They met at the home of their mutual friend Lois Curtis, and Lois's 15-year-old son George waited impatiently in the hallway outside the parlor to hear what her answer would be. Four agonizing hours went by while she tried to decide whether to accept his offer. David's horse was cold and hungry and kept kicking at the front stoop, so every now and then David would rush out to try to calm the horse before returning to his conversation with Maria. Finally, at one o'clock in the morning, they emerged from the parlor. Maria had said yes.

This handsome portrait of David Lee Child was probably painted around the time of the Childs' wedding.

Despite this success, other things were not going well for David. The year 1828 was an election year, and John Quincy Adams was not a popular President. Adams believed in a strong federal government and rapid economic development, and he tried to secure federal funding for roads, canals, industries, scientific research, and a national university. Most Americans, however, saw no need for such innovations, and they felt more loyalty to their towns and states than to the federal government. Many thought Adams was aristocratic, elitist, and out of touch with their lives. Adams did distrust the political judgments of ordinary people. He believed that statesmen should rise above the petty enthusiasms of mass politics and plan for the long-term good of the country. He lost the 1828 election by a large margin to Andrew Jackson, who styled himself as a friend of the people.

David's *Massachusetts Journal* was closely associated with Adams, and as Adams's political fortunes fell, so did the *Journal's*. David was personally responsible for the paper's finances, so when expenses exceeded income, he had to make up the difference. Instead of trying to reduce expenses as subscriptions declined, he borrowed money to keep the *Journal* going. Before long he had borrowed $15,000—an almost unimaginable amount of money at a time when $300 was enough to support a person for a year.

David also had legal problems. He had accused two prominent Massachusetts politicians of corruption, but—in his typical, careless fashion—he had failed to confirm the details before publishing the accusations. The men he accused were both affiliated with Andrew Jackson, so the Jacksonites concluded that David was playing dirty politics in an election year. They accused him of libel, and David faced hundreds of dollar's worth of legal fees and the possibility of huge fines or imprisonment.

When David confessed these new problems to Maria, she suggested that it might be prudent to postpone their wedding. On second thought, however, she decided that her earnings from the *Miscellany* were almost enough to support both of them, especially since she had already bought the furnishings for their new home. They were married in Watertown on Sunday, October 19, 1828. Maria wore a wedding gown of India muslin trimmed with white satin, and a large group of family and friends consumed 35 pounds of wedding cake.

The next day the Childs set up housekeeping in a tiny rented house. When George Curtis came to dinner a few weeks later, he noticed that they ate frugally. Maria made a meat pie and served baked potatoes and Indian pudding made from cornmeal. "There was no dessert, and no wine, no beverage of any kind but water, not even a cup of tea or coffee," George commented. But the young couple seemed happy and cheerful.

Most 19th-century men expected women to attend to homes and children and leave the "public" world of work and politics to men, but David was different. He always appreciated Maria's sharp intelligence and insightful comments, and he encouraged her to continue to learn and explore and form her own opinions about the pressing questions of their time. Under David's influence Maria became more knowledgeable about politics, while he became more knowledgeable about literature and Native American cultures.

Maria also continued to work. She, not David, was the one with an established profession and income, and she mostly supported the two of them by editing the *Miscellany* and writing books and short stories. She contributed regularly to the *Massachusetts Journal* and took responsibility for its literary columns, where she published several of her stories in an attempt to expand the paper's readership. She also did all the cooking and cleaning and sewing and mending, so she was very busy indeed.

Maria's influence on the *Journal* can be seen in its changed attitudes toward Indians. For almost 30 years, the federal government had tried to make all Indians leave the United States and move west of the Mississippi River. Earlier Presidents, including Thomas Jefferson, James Monroe, and John Quincy Adams, had insisted that the Indians be persuaded to sell their lands before they moved, but Andrew Jackson—who had gained quite a reputation as an "Indian fighter"—had no qualms about taking their land outright. He believed the Indians had no right to eastern lands, and he was willing to back his belief with guns and bullets.

The situation first came to a crisis in Georgia, where the Cherokee Indians not only owned 15 million acres of land but also had largely adopted the culture of their white neighbors. They grew cotton and fruit trees, herded sheep, published their own newspaper (written in both English and Cherokee), practiced Christianity, and even had their own constitution. No one could accuse them of being savages, and they wanted to stay where they had established farms and towns. In 1802, however, the federal government had promised Georgia that it would "extinguish existing Indian land title in the state." As the white population grew, and the demand for land intensified, white Georgians insisted that the federal government live up to its promise.

David protested in the *Journal* against physical attacks on the Cherokee, but he accepted whites' underlying assumption that Indians were doomed to extinction—that, in his words, "these native proprietors must disappear from the scenes of human action." Maria, in contrast, believed that Indians and whites could coexist peaceably and that Indians should have the same political and civil rights as whites. Injustice towards Native Americans, she argued, was intolerable in a republic founded on the principle that all people have a right to life, liberty, and property. When whites refused to acknowledge Indian land claims—or, worse, when they embraced Jackson's policy of extermination— they undermined the basic values of their country. Soon after the Childs' marriage, the *Journal* changed its editorial stance to support the Cherokee land claims and, more broadly, the rights of all Indians to life and to the land they had cultivated.

Nevertheless, the Childs and others like them were unable to turn the tide of anti-Indian sentiment. By 1837 federal troops were rounding up Cherokees and holding them in stockades. The following year, 15,000 Cherokees were forced to walk to the Indian Territory in what is now Oklahoma. About a quarter of them died along the way, on what they called the Trail of Tears. Jackson promised that

text continues on page 36

South Boston in the distance.

A Pier for boots, at Cottage Place, in Boston,
Where we lived from 1832 to 1835, in a very small cottage,
with a very small garden filled with flowers. The
sea dashed under the windows, and was often sparkling
with moon-beams when we went to bed. We used to
call the humble little home Le Paradis des Pauvres.

Maria sketched the view from her waterfront home in Boston. She and David used to call this house "Le Paradis des Pauvres" (French for "The Paradise of Paupers").

THE ART OF HOUSEKEEPING

In The Frugal Housewife *(1829), Lydia Maria Child urged readers to use all their resources carefully, plan ahead as much as possible, and keep every member of the family, including young children, busy doing something productive. She assumed that her audience already knew a lot about housewifery: as with her "recipe" for brewing beer, many of her directions would be of little use to a modern reader. In one of her tips, offered below, she specified that readers should use* New England *rum to wash their hair—not the Caribbean rum made from slave-grown crops.*

The true economy of housekeeping is simply the art of gathering up all the fragments, so that nothing be lost. I mean fragments of *time,* as well as *materials.* Nothing should be thrown away so long as it is possible to make any use of it, however trifling that use may be; and whatever the size of the family, every member should be employed either in earning or saving money.

"Time is money." For this reason, cheap as stockings are, it is good economy to knit them. Cotton and woolen yarn are both cheap; hose that are knit wear twice as long as woven ones; and they can be done at odd minutes of time, which would not be otherwise employed. Where there are children, or aged people, it is sufficient to recommend knitting, that it is an *employment.* . . .

In this country, we are apt to let children romp away their existence, till they get to be thirteen or fourteen. This is not well. It is not well for the purses and patience of parents; and it has a still worse effect on the morals and habits of the children. *Begin early* is the great maxim for everything in education. A child of six years old can be made useful; and should be taught to consider every day lost in which some little thing has not been done to assist others.

Children can very early be taught to take all the care of their own clothes.

They can knit garters, suspenders, and stockings; they can make patchwork and braid straw; they can make mats for the table, and mats for the floor; they can weed the garden, and pick cranberries from the meadow, to be carried to market. . . .

[I]t is a great deal better for the boys and girls on a farm to be picking blackberries at six cents a quart, than to be wearing out their clothes in useless play. They enjoy themselves just as well; and they are earning something to buy clothes, at the same time they are tearing them. . . .

In winter, always set the handle of your pump as high as possible, before you go to bed. Except in very frigid weather, this keeps the handle from freezing. When there is reason to apprehend extreme cold, do not forget to throw a rug or horse-blanket over your pump; a frozen pump is a comfortless preparation for a winter's breakfast. . . .

There should always be a heavy stone on the top of your pork, to keep it down [in its barrel of brine]. This stone is an excellent place to keep a bit of fresh meat in the summer, when you are afraid of its spoiling.

Have all the good bits of vegetables and meat collected after dinner, and minced before they are set away; that they may be in readiness to make a little savoury mince meat for supper or breakfast. . . .

Beer is a good family drink. A handful of hops, to a pailful of water, and a half-pint of molasses, makes good hop beer. Spruce mixed with hops is pleasanter than hops alone. Boxberry, fever-bush, sweet fern, and horseradish make a good and healthy diet-drink. The winter evergreen, or rheumatism weed, thrown in, is very beneficial to humours. Be careful not to mistake kill-lamb for winter-evergreen; they resemble each other. . . .

Too frequent use of an ivory comb injures the hair. Thorough combing, washing in suds, or N. E. [New England] rum, and thorough brushing, will keep it in order; and the washing does not injure the hair, as is generally supposed.

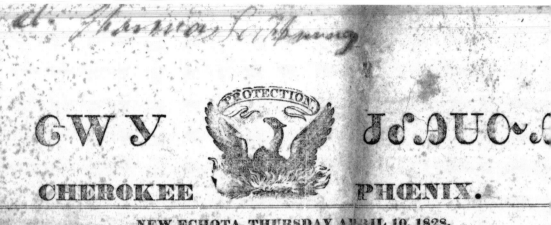

The Cherokee Indian Sequoia invented a syllabary so that his language could be written down and his people could send each other letters and publish newspapers in their native tongue.

text continued from page 32

their land rights in the Indian Territory would be secure, but other groups of Indians arrived every few years after being driven off their own lands, and in 1889 Oklahoma was opened to white settlers as well.

Fighting for Indian rights was not a good way to make a living, so Maria also turned her pen to more practical purposes. In 1829 she published the first edition of *The Frugal Housewife,* a domestic advice manual that became enormously popular. Previous cookbooks and domestic manuals were aimed at the upper classes, but Maria dedicated hers to "those who are not ashamed of economy." She wrote for "middling" women who did not have servants, running water, or other conveniences and who had to make a small income stretch as far as possible. Drawing on the lessons she had learned from her sister Mary back in Norridgewock, she gave directions for "Cheap Common Cooking," home remedies for illnesses ranging from toothache to ringworm to cancer, and a multitude of tips for preserving foods, taking care of clothing and home furnishings, and generally saving every possible penny.

The Frugal Housewife was reprinted 12 times in three years and eventually had more than 30 editions. Many reviewers felt that the book betrayed an unladylike obsession with money, and Maria's old friend Nathaniel Willis scathingly denounced its "thorough-going, unhesitating, cordial freedom from taste." But brisk sales proved that many readers appreciated the book's economical approach to housekeeping. Maria not only became nationally known as an authority about domestic affairs, but also earned more than $2,000 in just two years.

This money was much needed because David's troubles continued. In February 1830 he lost one of his libel suits and was sentenced to six months in jail. Maria decided that she could not afford to keep the house, so she sold some of her furniture and went to live with friends. Three times a day she took David's meals to the jail, because the prisoners were not given food. She alone edited the *Miscellany* and the *Journal,* and she also took a teaching job—work that she detested and that left her exhausted at the end of each day. By the time David was released, her health had deteriorated and rich friends insisted on taking her to the ocean until she felt better. Maria, however, was eager to return to David. "My dear husband," she wrote to him, "I *cannot* stay away a week. We lost a great deal of life by not being married sooner, and I am determined to waste no more precious hours of happiness."

This illustration from The Frugal House-wife *diagrammed the different cuts of meat, sending the implicit message that every part of an animal could be eaten. A frugal housewife, as Child always was, would buy the cheapest cuts and cook them in a way that made them palatable, but perhaps not delicious.*

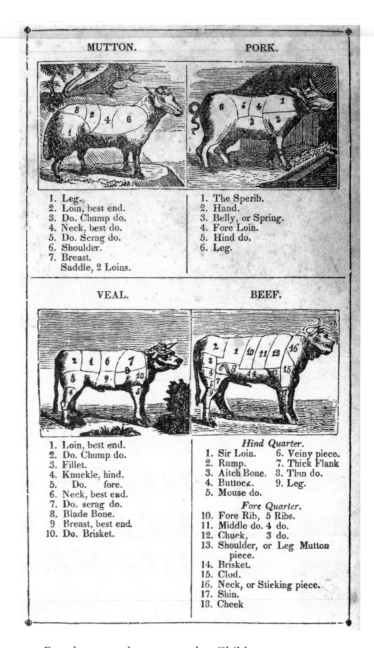

MUTTON.

1. Leg.
2. Loin, best end.
3. Do. Chump do.
4. Neck, best do.
5. Do. Scrag do.
6. Shoulder.
7. Breast.
   Saddle, 2 Loins.

PORK.

1. The Sperib.
2. Hand.
3. Belly, or Spring.
4. Fore Loin.
5. Hind do.
6. Leg.

VEAL.

1. Loin, best end.
2. Do. Chump do.
3. Fillet.
4. Knuckle, hind.
5. Do. fore.
6. Neck, best end.
7. Do. scrag do.
8. Blade Bone.
9. Breast, best end.
10. Do. Brisket.

BEEF.

Hind Quarter.

1. Sir Loin.   6. Veiny piece.
2. Rump.   7. Thick Flank
3. Aitch Bone. 8. Thin do.
4. Buttock.   9. Leg.
5. Mouse do.

Fore Quarter.

10. Fore Rib, 5 Ribs.
11. Middle do. 4 do.
12. Chuck,   3 do.
13. Shoulder, or Leg Mutton piece.
14. Brisket.
15. Clod.
16. Neck, or Sticking piece.
17. Shin.
18. Cheek

For the next three years the Childs were too poor to rent a home of their own. Most of their income went to pay off David's debts, and they moved from room to room every few months. At times Maria felt discouraged. She wanted to have a home, she wanted to become a mother, and she wanted to escape her "perpetual struggle with poverty." None of these goals seemed likely. Still, she did not regret her marriage. "In all that relates to external circumstances," she acknowledged to David, "our married life has been a stormy journey. But in all other respects, my dear husband, have we not realized all, and *more* than we then hoped?" And when Maria did feel disappointed by her life, she might remind herself that she was very well off indeed compared to a group of people who had even fewer rights than the Cherokee: the American slaves.

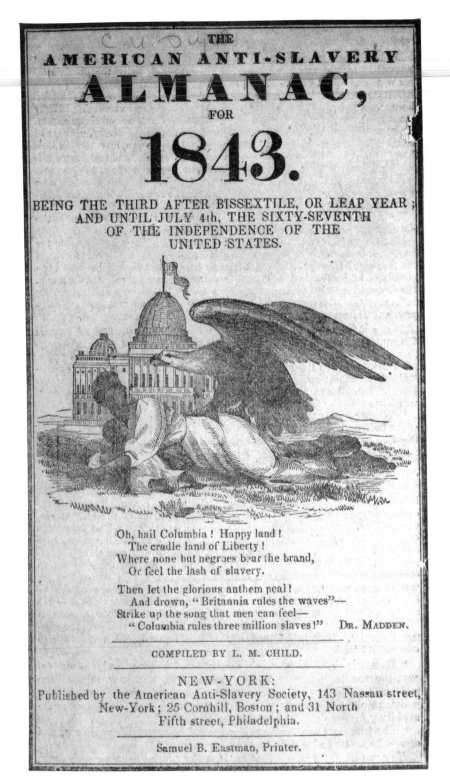

A slave woman shields her child from the American eagle on the cover of the 1843 American Anti-Slavery Almanac, *which Child edited. Child's writings often used patriotic images for ironic effect when she felt the country was betraying the principles it celebrated.*

3

THE ABOLITIONIST CRUSADE

Like most Northerners in the 1820s, Maria Child felt uncomfortable with the idea of slavery, but she was even more uncomfortable with the idea of slaves being freed. In one of her early stories, a young boy discovers the existence of slavery and exclaims, "The people at the southward must be very cruel, or they would not keep slaves as they do." His aunt—the voice of reason—tells him that slaveholders are not to blame for "the curse of slavery." The slaves, she explains, have become unaccustomed to liberty and cannot take care of themselves. Good masters therefore educate and care for their slaves, give freedom to those who deserve it, and patiently wait for a time when slavery can be safely eliminated. Child did not suggest *how* such a situation might come about, except by encouraging masters to voluntarily prepare their slaves for freedom—which, of course, very few did.

Child's views began to change in June 1830, when she met William Lloyd Garrison. Garrison was trying to start an abolitionist movement but had so far found little success. After reading and admiring Child's writings, he believed that she could help him mobilize popular opinion—if she wanted to. He therefore sought her out during a brief visit to Boston.

Slavery, Garrison argued to anyone who would listen, was an unmitigated evil that should be abolished immediately, not vaguely and gradually at some point in the future. Some blacks were ignorant, he acknowledged, but they could be educated, and other blacks were just as intelligent and capable as any whites. Justice therefore required nothing less than the abolition of slavery and the elimination of racial discrimination. Blacks should not have to wait any longer for the economic, political, and civil rights that were their due.

Most people considered Garrison a crackpot, but Child's own thinking about Indians forced her to take his arguments seriously. She believed that Native Americans should not be treated differently from white people—that they should have the same rights to live and own land. Why then, Garrison asked her, did she accept the enslavement of people whose ancestors happened to have been born in Africa? Garrison "got hold of the strings of my conscience," Child later remembered. He made her feel that it was intolerable to live in a country that deprived any of its people of the basic rights to earn money, decide how to spend it, and live with their families in peace without fear of a wife or husband or child being sold away at a master's whim.

Even after this momentous conversation, Child had many questions. What would happen, she asked, if slavery were suddenly eradicated? Would former

Driven by passionate Christian faith and radical anti-racism, William Lloyd Garrison was determined to give slaves the same opportunity for social mobility that he had been given.

slaves and former slaveholders face economic ruin? Would blacks turn violently against their former owners, perhaps murdering them all? Were blacks really biologically inferior to whites, as those in favor of slavery argued, and could they ever become fully equal members of American society? Furthermore, was slavery really so bad? Masters had a large economic investment in their slaves; would they really put that investment at risk by treating slaves poorly? How common was cruelty? Did the Northern states or the federal government have any legal right to intervene in the laws and practices of the Southern states?

Answers to these questions were difficult to find. Most people accepted slavery and did not think much about it. No one had really studied slavery, its consequences, or what happened in places where slaves had been emancipated—such as the Northern states of the United States or the Caribbean island of Hispaniola. Child therefore had to answer her questions for herself. For three years she read everything she could find that was related to slavery and emancipation. Finally, in 1833, she published a synthesis of her findings as *An Appeal in Favor of that Class of Americans Called Africans.*

The *Appeal* proved that Garrison's early impressions of Child were correct. She could make people listen to abolitionist ideas in a way he could not. Most people did not like what they heard, but some were inspired. Future senator Charles Sumner and reformer Wendell Phillips became two of the most influential leaders of the abolitionist movement after they read Child's book, while hundreds, even thousands, of other readers contributed to the movement in more modest ways.

In the *Appeal,* Child argued that slavery is terribly destructive to all concerned, even slave owners. Slaves experienced degradation at best and cruelty and murder at worst. More broadly, the South's economy was dragged down by the

text continues on page 46

A MATTER OF DUTY

Child's overarching goal in An Appeal in Favor of That Class of Americans
Called Africans *(1833) was to persuade white Northerners to act against slavery. To
achieve this goal she used a combination of personal anecdotes (which roused moral
indignation against the cruelty of slavery) and rational arguments (which insisted that
free labor was both safer and more productive than slave labor). She also emphasized
the special vulnerability of slave women. The second passage below delicately refers to
rape, while the third describes a slave woman dying after she went into labor (became
"ill") while on a late-pregnancy errand for her master. Genteel nineteenth-century
ladies did not write about sex, rape, pregnancy, or childbirth, so Child's language was
euphemistic, but she expected readers to share her outrage. She did not, however, let
Northerners feel superior to Southerners: white racism, she argued, was the foundation
of slavery, and Northerners were at least as racist as Southerners.*

It is said that when the first pack of blood-hounds arrived in St. Domingo
[Haiti], the white planters delivered to them the first negro they found,
merely by way of experiment; and when they saw him immediately torn in
pieces, they were delighted to find the dogs so well trained in their business. . . .

The negro woman is unprotected either by law or public opinion. She is
the property of her master, and her daughters are his property. They are
allowed to have no conscientious scruples, no sense of shame, no regard for
the feelings of husband, or parent; they must be entirely subservient to the
will of their owner, on pain of being whipped as near death as will comport
with his interest, or quite to death, if it suit his pleasure.

Those who know human nature would be able to conjecture the
unavoidable result, even if it were not betrayed by the amount of mixed population. . . . [I]t is indeed a strange state of society where the father sells his
child, and the brother puts his sister up at auction! . . .

A planter had occasion to send a female slave some distance on an
errand. She did not return so soon as he expected, and he grew angry. At

last he gave orders that she should be severely whipped when she came back. When the poor creature arrived, she pleaded for mercy, saying she had been so very ill, that she was obliged to rest in the fields; but she was ordered to receive another dozen of lashes, for having had the impudence to speak. She died at the whipping post; nor did she perish alone—a new born baby died with her. . . .

Our prejudice against the blacks is founded in sheer pride; and it originates in the circumstance that people of their color only, are universally allowed to be slaves. We made slavery, and slavery makes the prejudice. No Christian, who questions his own conscience, can justify himself in indulging the feeling. The removal of this prejudice is not a matter of opinion—it is a matter of *duty*. . . .

The condition of this people in ancient times is very far from indicating intellectual or moral inferiority.—Ethiopia held a conspicuous place among the nations.—Her princes were wealthy and powerful, and her people distinguished for integrity and wisdom. Even the proud Grecians evinced respect for Ethiopia. . . .

While we bestow our earnest disapprobation on the system of slavery, let us not flatter ourselves that we are in reality any better than our brethren of the South. . . . Our prejudice against colored people is even more inveterate than it is at the South. The planter is often attached to his negroes, and lavishes caresses and kind words upon them, as he would on a favorite hound: but our cold-hearted, ignoble prejudice admits of no exception—no intermission. . . . Those who are kind and liberal on all other subjects, unite with the selfish and the proud in their unrelenting efforts to keep the colored population in the lowest state of degradation; and the influence they unconsciously exert over children early infuses into their innocent minds the same strong feelings of contempt.

text continued from page 43

inefficiency of slave labor, by white people's unwillingness to do hard physical work—which was associated with being a slave—and by the constant fear of slave rebellions. Southern states had to enact ever harsher laws in order to keep the slaves under control. These laws impinged on whites as well as blacks. If a white woman taught a black child to read, she risked criminal prosecution; if a white man emancipated his slaves, he lost them as workers and neighbors as well. Child believed that such laws threatened to undermine the country's traditions of freedom. If people became accustomed to surrendering their civil liberties for the sake of an oppressive social order, then whites too could no longer appeal to the ideals of freedom and justice to protect themselves from injustices.

The only solution, Child concluded, was emancipation. "Slavery causes insurrections," she warned, "while emancipation prevents them." In Saint-Domingue (now Haiti), she pointed out, slaves had rebelled against their masters in 1791, but after they achieved freedom, they worked hard, lived peaceably with whites, and set about building a stable society. When the French ruler Napoléon tried to restore slavery in the colony in 1802, however, blacks almost eliminated whites from the island. Such violence contrasted with the earlier period of peace after the slaves won their freedom and also with the experience of the Northern states, which had freed slaves after the American Revolution without a single instance of bloodshed. History, Child concluded, proves that slavery leads to mounting violence, while voluntary emancipation leads to peace and economic development.

Even more radically, Child insisted that emancipation alone was not enough to establish liberty and justice for blacks. Racial prejudice had to be eliminated, too—and in this matter Northerners were no more virtuous than Southerners. Child documented Northern violence against blacks and discrimination in schools, jobs, housing, churches, transportation facilities, and inns and hotels. She even criticized the "unjust law" that prohibited marriage between people of different colors. A man, she argued, should have just as much freedom to choose a wife as to choose a religion. In both North and South, she concluded, blacks were penned in by a network of racist laws and prejudices that kept them from obtaining education, improving themselves and their children, and becoming fully equal members of American society.

At the time, very few people imagined that blacks might ever become full Americans. Whites who hoped to eliminate slavery usually assumed that the freed slaves would go "back" to Africa—even if they, and their parents and grandparents, had been born in the United States. The American Colonization Society sent freed slaves to Liberia, an African country that had been created for the purpose of receiving former American slaves, and most white people believed that emancipation would require systematic deportation of the freed people.

Most blacks, however, wanted to stay in the country where they were born, not go to a continent they had never seen, and Child took their side. The very title of her *Appeal* asserted that blacks are a "Class of Americans"—not foreigners. Colonizationists assumed that racial prejudice was inevitable, and most of them believed that blacks were biologically inferior to whites and therefore could never become equal members of an integrated society. Child marshaled an enormous amount of data to show that black people are intellectually and morally equal to whites. She wrote about Africa's ancient civilizations, the achievements of individual blacks in the United States, and the successful republic in Haiti. In every way she could think of, she insisted that racial prejudice had no legitimate ground and that blacks and whites could and should learn to live together as equals—even, if they wanted to, as husbands and wives.

These were radical ideas in the 1830s, and the *Appeal* produced a storm of outrage. Southerners and Northerners alike were offended by Child's portraits of their regions and indignant at her calls for change. The newspapers were full of critical reviews and angry refutations. The prominent Colonizationist minister Leonard Bacon, for example, disputed Child's claim that racism was rampant in the North. "If Mrs. Child has any confessions [of her own] to make, very well," he wrote scornfully, "only...let her not attempt to impute the same guilt to the public sentiment of New England." Child's older brother James was more blunt: he told her he despised both "niggers" and "nigger-lovers." Many of Child's friends, including her mentor George Ticknor, refused to see her. Even Child's beloved brother Convers told his sister that her views were too extreme and counseled moderation.

Worst of all, readers stopped buying Child's other writings. Sales of *The Frugal Housewife* plummeted and the rest of Child's books went out of print. Parents canceled their children's subscriptions to the *Juvenile Miscellany,* and within months the magazine had folded. Although the *Appeal* sold reasonably well—it was, after all, notorious—Child found herself with almost no source of income. David's *Massachusetts Journal* had folded at the beginning of 1832, leaving him only an enormous pile of debts.

Other early activists faced similar problems, or worse. Child knew well the story of Prudence Crandall, a Quaker woman in Connecticut who had enrolled a few black girls in her school. Her neighbors were horrified that New England might become "the Liberia of America"—a place where blacks would go to try to improve their lives. They poured manure in Crandall's well, set fire to her school, and refused to allow Crandall and her teachers and students to buy groceries or get medical care. Child dedicated her *Appeal* to Samuel May, who was leading Crandall's defense in two legal trials. After the judge declared that free blacks have no citizenship rights, and a mob destroyed her school with a battering ram, Crandall gave up and fled to Illinois.

Despite such violent opposition, Child became more and more involved in the abolitionist movement. The *Appeal*'s careful research and rational but passionate analysis converted many readers to abolitionism, and they naturally looked to its author for guidance about what to do next. Child met personally or corresponded with many activists, plotting strategies and helping them see how they could contribute to the cause. She also met with people who she hoped would become activists—such as the influential Boston minister William Ellery Channing—and in several cases convinced them to support the abolitionist movement. She wrote several more antislavery books, stories, and articles in an attempt to reach an ever-expanding range of people. She attended meetings of the American Anti-Slavery Society and the Boston Female Anti-Slavery Society, raised money to support their publications, and helped organize large public meetings when abolitionist lecturers came to town.

Violence against abolitionists erupted in several major cities in 1835, which became known as the "mob year." Both Garrison and George Thompson narrowly escaped being lynched. Thompson, an Englishman and powerful orator, was credited with persuading the British people to support the abolition of slavery in the West Indies. He came to the United States in 1834 to see whether he could work the same magic here, and he and Child soon became close friends. American newspapers denounced him as a foreign troublemaker, and angry mobs appeared wherever he went. The Childs frequently helped protect him: they would watch for gathering mobs, distract his pursuers, or spirit him away to stay in the back room of a friend's home until it was safe for him to appear on the street again. Once Child and a group of other abolitionist women surrounded Thompson and guided him to a secret back exit, where a carriage was waiting for him, as a lecture hall filled with angry men armed with clubs and whips.

A DOWNRIGHT GABBLER,
or a goose that deserves to be hissed—

Newspapers were scathing in their criticisms of Fanny Wright, the first woman to lecture in public in the United States. Although Wright's lectures were well attended, many people came to gawk and heckle rather than listen.

There was one thing Child refused to do, even for the abolitionist cause: she would not speak in front of a group that contained men. At that time, no American woman had spoken to a mixed-sex—or, in their language, "promiscuous"—public assembly. Child publicly disapproved when an Englishwoman, Fanny Wright, went on a lecture tour to support a variety of reform causes, including gradual emancipation of slaves. Child felt that public speaking was indelicate for a woman, and she was intensely embarrassed whenever someone suggested she do it. At one meeting her colleague Lewis Tappan tried to get her to speak. "You really ought to make an effort to overcome your reluctance," he admonished her, "when you reflect how much good you can do." When Child continued to refuse, Tappan turned to her husband and tried to convince him to order his wife to speak to the group. David replied that he wished his wife "to act in perfect freedom" and the topic was finally dropped. Child was frustrated by meetings in which abolitionist men were long-winded and indecisive, and infuriated by public debates in which her colleagues let the ridiculous arguments of pro-slavery men go unchallenged, but she never spoke up. "Oh, if I were a man," she wrote to a friend, "how I *would* lecture! But I am a woman, and so I sit in the corner and knit socks." Child did a lot more than just knit socks, but she always felt that her actions had to be ladylike.

A new opportunity seemed to open up when Thompson arranged for the Childs to work in England as agents for a British antislavery society. Child would write and David would speak, and both of them would meet informally with people who might be able to help the abolitionist cause. Child was ecstatic about the opportunity to travel abroad and earn a small salary while doing work she deeply believed in. She was also personally relieved: she was still writing, but because of her abolitionist activities, her works were not selling well and she needed another source of income. Two days before their departure Child held an auction of all her household furnishings. She boarded a ship to New York, where she and David would transfer to a ship bound for England, with a light heart.

Her spirits fell, however, when David was arrested in New York. One of his former partners, George Snelling, had sued him for debts associated with the ill-fated *Massachusetts Journal* and obtained an injunction forbidding David to leave the country. The ship sailed without them while Child sat on the dock and cried. The court case dragged on for four years, disrupting many other plans, until a judge finally decreed that David owed Snelling $9,750—on top of all his other debts.

Once again, Child gathered herself together and tried to go on. Now without any furniture, she and David rented a room from their friends Joseph and Margaret Carpenter. The Carpenters lived on an isolated farm in New Rochelle, New York. Their house was a stop on the Underground Railroad, the network of homes and churches that helped slaves escape to the North. They also had taken in three orphaned black children, and Child enjoyed the novel experience of living in an interracial household. Black and white members of the household (including black and white servants) all ate at the same table—a shocking arrangement by the standards of the time. "It is a solid satisfaction," Child wrote to her friend Ellis Loring, "to see prejudice so entirely forgotten." The local school became integrated when Child took the children there and stayed until she was sure they would be welcomed—an act that took a great deal of courage after Prudence Crandall's ordeal. One white family withdrew its child from the school, but otherwise the black children were accepted without difficulties.

Meanwhile, the Childs tried to decide what to do next. David liked the idea of moving to Mexico, where a friend was trying to create a racially integrated settlement, but Child detested the thought of living on a distant frontier. The question was settled for them when pro-slavery Texans conquered that part of Mexico, but David soon shifted his attention to Illinois, another frontier area.

Child still hoped to cross the Atlantic, so she was delighted when she and David were again invited to go to England, this time to edit a new abolitionist newspaper. Her books were selling well in England—sometimes better than in the United States—and English magazines were eager for contributions from a prominent American writer. This time, however, David showed uncharacteristic financial caution: he insisted on a guaranteed income, and without that he refused to go. Child yearned to see another country and meet European literary figures, and believed (probably rightly) that a few years abroad would reinvigorate her writing career, but David was adamant. As it turned out, Child would never leave the United States.

David was soon excited by a new possibility: growing sugar beets. Almost all of the sugar sold in the United States came from sugarcane grown by slaves, and abolitionists were eager to find an alternative source of sweetening. Sugarcane could not grow in the North, but sugar beets could. Unfortunately, very few Americans knew how to turn beets into sugar, and they kept it a closely guarded commercial secret. David heard that a new business, the Illinois Beet Sugar Company, was looking for someone to travel to France and Belgium, learn how to grow and process beets, and establish sugar manufacturing in Illinois. He thought this was a perfect opportunity. He could help the abolitionist cause, make money, use his language skills, and travel to Europe on his own account, not as the escort of his more-famous wife.

So David went off to Europe alone, while Child moved in with her father and later stayed with other friends in Boston. Being left behind was a bitter disappointment. "My poverty, but not my will," she explained in a letter to David's mother, "consented to remaining behind, while one I loved so much was going where I so much wished to go." Even worse, Child began to suspect that David no longer loved her. During his first six months abroad, he sent her only three, as she put it, "rather business like" letters. The first letter contained not a single word of affection—just practical matters that he wanted her to take care of.

Child missed David terribly, and for the first time in her life suffered from writer's block. She stopped writing, stopped publishing, and sank into a deep depression. She often felt that it was useless to try to accomplish anything and spent most days in a listless gloom. All her plans and dreams, it seemed, had come to nothing. She was, she confessed to Louisa Loring, "out of sorts with matrimony"—and David's infrequent and impersonal letters, and refusal to say when he might come home, suggested that he was, too.

Many abolitionist women felt that they had a special responsibility to speak up for slave women. Slave women often worked in the fields while men were at leisure. Child was no stranger to hard work, but she shared the critical attitudes in Benjamin Latrobe's painting, "An Overseer Doing His Duty."

One bright spot in this otherwise bleak year was the Anti-Slavery Convention of American Women that met in New York in May 1837. This meeting was doubly historic: it was the first time women held a public political meeting in the United States, and it was the first substantial interracial convention of any kind. Child was excited by the gathering, and she and Angelina Grimké (a South Carolina slaveholders' daughter who had become a Quaker abolitionist) were the most vocal members of the meeting: they presented the most resolutions and made the most daring arguments. Child even urged the women to oppose racial discrimination in employment, encourage black businesses, and eradicate social segregation—goals that would still be considered radical 120 years later.

Finally, more than a year after his departure, David came home. As Maria had feared, the Illinois Beet Sugar Company had ceased to exist when the gentlemen sponsoring it lost interest. Although David had been promised a good salary on top of his travel expenses, in actuality he received no money for his year's travels. Instead he had racked up more debts, not the least of which was for several hundred dollars' worth of beet-processing machinery that he bought on his own initiative. In the end, the machinery would rust on the docks of New York, while Child paid for it out of her now-meager royalties from *The Frugal Housewife*.

More and more, Child began to think that David was responsible for much of his "bad luck." He was careless with details, too willing to trust other people, and an incurable procrastinator. Somehow, he seemed to think that any problem could be solved by more money—which always meant more debt. Child was determined not to be dependent on anyone, so when she stayed with a friend she insisted on paying for her food if she possibly could. David, in contrast, seemed to think nothing of borrowing thousands of dollars even when he had no idea how to pay back the thousands he already owed.

Nevertheless, when David decided to move to Northampton, Massachusetts, to set up a beet farm of his own, Child went with him. Predictably, the land David rented had been overused and was no longer fertile. It took an enormous amount of labor, and a lot of money for machines, to produce a small quantity of the experimental sugar, so once again David was going deeper into debt. Child often spent six or eight hours a day helping David in the fields, in addition to doing all the cooking, cleaning, and sewing for three people after her father moved in with them. She still could not find the creativity to write, so she tried to find other ways of making money (editing, candy making, hand-coloring maps for a publisher), but nothing worked out. All of her energy went to survival, scrabbling each day's meals out of whatever she could grow or find.

Child quickly discovered that Northampton was politically and socially conservative and a very poor place for her to make friends. The town was a popular summer vacation spot for rich Southerners, who would usually bring a few slaves with them, so the Childs' abolitionist views were intensely unpopular with both visitors and natives.

One summer Child became friendly with a slave named Rosa, who explained that her old mistress, who had died, had promised her and her children freedom, but the heirs had conveniently "lost" the will. Rosa was trying to decide what to do next. Massachusetts law let her claim her freedom as soon as she entered the state, but if she did so, she would never see her children again. If she returned to the South, she would be a slave and she might be sold away from her children anyway. Child sympathized with Rosa's dilemma and was disappointed when she decided to return home—while her owner proudly boasted that the famous abolitionist had been unable to "coax" Rosa away from "her beloved mistress."

Finally, after two long and lonely years, Child saw a way to escape the drudgery of farm life and the isolation of what she called the "iron-bound Valley of the Connecticut."

The American Anti-Slavery Society had started an abolitionist newspaper in New York, and it needed a new editor.
The Childs were invited to edit the newspaper together,
with the understanding that David would remain in
Northampton and grow beets and contribute occasional
editorials, while Child would move to New York and actually manage the paper. Their salary would be $1,000 a year.

Child hated to leave David, but she hated poverty and
living in Northampton even more, so she accepted the
offer. The masthead of the *National Anti-Slavery Standard*
soon declared that Lydia Maria Child was the editor and
David Lee Child the assistant editor—a remarkable role
reversal in a time when men were expected to be in charge
of everything.

Indeed, Child was the first woman ever to edit a political
newspaper, but she did not even think about letting that stop
her. The women's rights movement was just beginning, and
Child knew most of its leaders personally, but she was
ambivalent about women claiming rights for themselves.
She thought that women should help others and should not
limit their efforts because they were women. It is best, she
explained, "not to *talk* about our right, but simply go forward and *do* whatsoever we deem a duty." If editing a political
newspaper would help slaves and put bread on the table,
then she would edit a political newspaper.

Furthermore, Child did not want the *Standard* to be
only a political paper. The abolitionist movement, she
believed, needed to expand its numbers by reaching out to
people who were not already committed to its cause. In
addition to political reports and tactical advice, therefore,
she published travelogues, short stories, and essays that
appealed to more general readers. She reprinted, for example, all of *Jonathan Jefferson Whitlaw,* a novel written by the
Englishwoman Frances Trollope and set in the slaveholding
Southwest. Child's goal was to help readers imagine what
life in a slave society was like—to appeal to "imagination

and taste"—and then gradually lead them to think about how they could help eradicate slavery.

Child's strategy for expanding readership was remarkably successful. When she took it over, the *Standard* had 1,500 subscribers. A year later, it had 4,000 subscribers, and a year after that, 5,000. Because four people on average read every copy, Child was actually reaching 20,000 people every week.

One of Child's practices, however, probably did not help expand circulation. As she had earlier in her *Appeal,* Child tried to combat Northern racism as well as Southern slavery. She reported on blacks who died of exposure after being refused a seat inside a stagecoach or ship cabin because of the color of their skin. She decried the hypocrisy of taxing blacks to help pay for public schools, then refusing them admission to those schools while criticizing them for being uneducated. She proved that some blacks were educated by publishing articles by black writers, including the former slave and abolitionist Frederick Douglass. She even wrote about the years of the Middle Ages when Anglo-Saxons in England were slaves of the Norman invaders, and she argued that whites and blacks responded in the same ways

For many slaves, the threat of being sold off and permanently separated from family members was an ever-present shadow. Separation was particularly likely when an owner died, and husbands, wives, and children might be sold or distributed to different heirs with no thought for their family ties.

to conditions of slavery. All races, Child insisted, have similar virtues and similar flaws.

Child's antiracist stance—though controversial—was not nearly as dangerous to the paper as the intellectual and political divisions within the abolitionist movement. Some abolitionists believed racial equality would require a transformation of how white people thought and felt; these abolitionists therefore focused on changing people's *ideas*. Other reformers believed that slavery was above all a legal and political institution; they therefore focused on building political strength and changing *laws*. Some believed that abolitionists should "come out" from any institution that was tainted by slavery—such as churches and political parties—and that anyone who did not do so was a half-hearted hypocrite.

Others believed that activists would win their cause only by forming alliances with less committed people and that it was possible to believe in abolitionism without dedicating one's whole life to it. Some believed that abolitionism was part of a broader social movement toward freedom and equality for all people. Others believed that abolitionists should not be distracted from the goal of eradicating slavery by taking on other causes—such as antiracism or women's rights—as well. Some believed that women should do all they could to help the slaves. Others believed that women should stay within their traditional roles and not speak in public or help run meetings, no matter what.

The abolitionist societies split, and then split again, over these issues. Old friends and colleagues became bitter enemies. Sometimes people changed sides. Lewis Tappan—who had earlier urged Child to address a meeting—now helped organize a rival organization because the American Anti-Slavery Society voted to allow women to participate in its meetings. Every group, of course, wanted the *Standard* to support its views, so everyone wanted Child on their

On the title page of a collection of slaves' individual stories, Child represented Justice as a white woman holding the scales of justice in one hand and reaching out to unlock the chains of a slave woman with the other. "Am I not a woman and a sister?" the caption asked.

side. She tried to take a middle road, holding the movement together by emphasizing what abolitionists had in common rather than what divided them. Inevitably, however, any statement she made would infuriate someone.

Furthermore, the American Anti-Slavery Society was taking on more projects than it could afford, so most of the *Standard*'s subscription money went to purposes other than running the paper. Eventually the paper was $2,000 in debt, mostly to printers and paper sellers and other small businessmen who needed the money to support their families. Child refused to accept any salary when such debts were outstanding, so she lived on the charity of friends and survived for three months with only 37 1/2 ¢ in her pocket.

Once again, Child felt deeply disappointed and discouraged. The abolitionist movement was disintegrating because people attacked each other instead of finding ways to work together. Child tried to smooth the ruffled feathers, but every few weeks she was swept up into a crisis. After all her work, she was again poverty-stricken and dependent on friends for food and shelter. Not surprisingly, Child decided that it was time to leave the *Standard*.

In May 1843, Child wrote her last editorial. In the following year the *Standard*'s subscriptions plunged from 5,000 to 1,300. Clearly, despite all the complaints about how Child ran the paper, her talents were missed. But Child did not miss the factionalism that was tearing the abolitionist movement apart, and she distanced herself from the movement as much as she could. She no longer attended meetings, did fund-raising, or wrote abolitionist books or articles. If a big conference gathered where she lived, she would leave the city for a week in order to make sure she would not run into any former friends on the street. After so much turmoil, so much infighting, so much fruitless struggle, Child gave up on political activism. "I never again will join any association, for *any* purpose," she resolved, and she kept that resolution for the rest of her life.

Over the river, and through the wood—
When grandmother sees us come,
She will say, Oh dear,
The children are here,
Bring a pie for every one.

Over the river, and through the wood—
Now grandmother's cap I spy!
Hurra for the fun!
Is the pudding done?
Hurra for the pumpkin pie!

Child's best known lines are from a much-loved Thanksgiving poem: "Over the river and through the woods / To grandfather's house we go; / The horse knows the way, / To carry the sleigh, / Through the white and drifted snow." This illustrated edition of "A New England Boy's Song" included both some less-famous later verses and a humorous drawing of an overwhelming pumpkin pie.

THE PURSUIT OF LITERARY EXCELLENCE

After so many bitter experiences, Maria Child decided that it was time to return to the love of her youth: writing. Disillusioned with all forms of overt activism, she still hoped that her writing might change minds and hearts. When her friend Francis Shaw criticized her for abandoning her social concerns, Child answered that she was not leaving behind her concerns, only the forms they had previously taken:

> Some...would convince me that I am doing very wrong not to attend reformatory meetings, to be on their committees, to draw up reports, help settle disputes, visit prisons, &c. But when I try to do these things, I feel that I am going out of my own life, into something which is to *me* artificial, and therefore false. My own appropriate mission is obviously that of a writer; and I am convinced that I can do more good...by working in that way; infusing, as I must necessarily do, *principles* in favor of peace, universal freedom, &c into all I write.

Fictional stories and personal essays, Child hoped, would promote the principles she believed in even better than formal organizations—and might also allow her to regain her literary reputation and climb back out of poverty. "Formed as my character now is," she concluded, "I cannot do otherwise than make literature the honest agent of my conscience and my heart."

First, though, Child had to distance herself from David. According to 19th-century law, a married woman had no economic existence apart from her husband. If she earned or inherited money, it belonged to him, not to her. David continued to float from one unsuccessful project to another, and his debts continued to grow. Finally, he filed for bankruptcy, and in June 1843 everything he owned was sold at auction. Child lost most of her clothing and all of her jewelry, including precious mementos given to her by friends and antislavery groups. Fortunately, her father already owned the rights to her books, which he had taken as security for some of the money he lent David, so she did not lose everything. She decided, however, that it was time to officially separate her financial affairs from David's, and David agreed "to part partnership, so far as *pecuniary* matters are concerned." Because Child could not, as a married woman, control her own money, her friend Ellis Loring became her financial guardian.

This was not a divorce, but it was the next thing to it. For nine years the couple lived separately. They occasionally spent a few weeks together, and Child cherished the small windows of domestic intimacy these visits provided. David, however, showed little interest in prolonging their visits or making them more frequent, and Child refused to let his decisions affect her plans in any way. David, she now believed, was fundamentally incapable of responsible behavior, and she resolved that she would no longer "*try* to help what did not admit of help." "I *cannot,*" she explained to Loring, "be agreeably situated while I am involved with David's destiny."

Child's psychological and physical separation from David allowed her literary career to blossom again. Back when she was editing the *Standard,* Child had published a weekly "Letter from New-York" about her experiences in the country's largest city. She loved to wander the streets, going places where respectable women usually did not venture—such as the Tombs, New York's notoriously dark and dirty prison, or the blocks where prostitutes gathered. In her columns, she compassionately described fugitive slaves, abused women, ill-treated prisoners, starving children living by their wits on the street, and the tragedies of racial and religious prejudice. Much crime, she argued, was caused by poverty, and society should do more to help its most desperate members rebuild their lives. But not all of Child's essays were about suffering and injustice: she also wrote of human sympathy, of music and art, and of the wonderful characters who gathered in city neighborhoods.

The *Standard's* readers loved these columns, and one of Child's first projects after she left the newspaper was to gather them into a book. Both readers and critics praised the collection, which sold briskly, and a second edition was needed only seven months after the first. From then on, Child found that publishers were much more willing to forgive her abolitionist taint and publish her work. She also, though she did not realize it, established a new genre of journalism. So many journalists followed her example that "city" columns—based on a writer's first-person experiences of city life—became a staple of urban newspapers.

During the next six years Child published eight more books, and her short stories and essays appeared in a wide variety of magazines and newspapers. She never regained her pre-*Appeal* popularity, but she was once again considered a solid, established writer. She earned enough to live simply but comfortably, and she could even save a little bit of money for the future.

Child loved these years in New York. The city was indisputably the cultural center of the country, and she delighted in its museums, concert halls, and opera houses. She befriended several young musicians, painters, sculptors, and actresses and

text continues on page 66

A CALL FOR EQUALITY

In some of her "Letters from New-York," Child wrote about a topic that she did not mention in her earlier published writings: the obstacles and injustices that white women confronted. In this excerpt from December 31, 1844, she describes the stunted life of a "genteel" young lady.

It is one of the saddest sights to see a young girl born of wealthy and worldly parents, full of heart and soul, her kindly impulses continually checked by etiquette, her noble energies repressed by genteel limitations. She must not presume to love anybody, till father and mother find a suitable match; she must not laugh loud, because it is vulgar; she must not walk fast, because it is ungenteel; she must not work in the garden, for fear the sun and wind may injure her complexion; she must sew nothing but gossamer, lest it mar the delicacy of her hands; she must not study, because gentlemen do not admire literary ladies. Thus left without ennobling objects of interest, the feelings and energies are usually concentrated on frivolous and unsatisfactory pursuits, and woman becomes a by-word and a jest, for her giddy vanity, her love of dress and beaux.

There is no measuring the mischief done by the prevailing tendency to teach women to be virtuous as a duty to man rather than to God—for the sake of pleasing the creature, rather than the Creator. "God is thy law, *thou* mine," said Eve to Adam. May Milton be forgiven for sending that thought "out into everlasting time" in such a jewelled setting. What weakness, vanity, frivolity, infirmity of moral purpose, sinful flexibility of principle—in a word, what soul-stifling, has been the result of thus putting man in the place of God!

"Letters from New-York" often combined detailed descriptions of the city, and even flowery flights of fancy, with sharp social commentary. In this column from February 17, 1842, Child outlined the social conditions that condemned so many children to poverty, ignorance, and crime.

The other day, I went forth for exercise merely, without other hope of enjoyment than a farewell to the setting sun, on the now deserted Battery, and a fresh kiss from the breezes of the sea, ere they passed through the polluted city, bearing healing on their wings. I had not gone far, when I met a little ragged urchin, about four years old, with a heap of newspapers, "more big as he could carry," under his little arm, and another clenched in his small, red fist. The sweet voice of childhood was prematurely cracked into shrillness, by screaming street cries, at the top of his lungs; and he looked blue, cold, and disconsolate.... Imagination followed him to the miserable cellar where he probably slept on dirty straw; I saw him flogged, after his day of cheerless toil, because he had failed to bring home pence enough for his parents' grog; I saw wicked ones come muttering and beckoning between his young soul and heaven; they tempted him to steal to avoid the dreaded beating. I saw him, years after, bewildered and frightened, in the police-office, surrounded by hard faces. Their law-jargon conveyed no meaning to his ear, awakened no slumbering moral sense, taught him no clear distinction between right and wrong; but from their cold, harsh tones, and heartless merriment, he drew the inference that they were enemies; and, as such, he hated them.... He tries the universal resort of weakness against force; if they are too strong for *him,* he will be too cunning for *them.* Their cunning is roused to detect his cunning: and thus the gallows-game is played....

When, O when, will men learn that society makes and cherishes the very crimes it so fiercely punishes, and *in* punishing reproduces?... God grant the little shivering carrier-boy a brighter destiny than I have foreseen for him.

text continued from page 63

took pleasure in helping them find work and establish their reputations. Any European artist who came to the United States came to New York, and the city was still small enough that Child could usually meet anyone she wanted to. Ole Bull, a Norwegian violinist, became a close friend after Child fell in love with his music during a concert. Child even bought a piano—quite an extravagance for her modest budget—and studied music theory. Several musicians were impressed by her understanding of their art, and some even played for her privately in her sitting room. Although Child still regretted that her trips to England had been snatched away from her, in New York she found the rich cultural life that fed her spirit.

She also found many friends. One important friend was the journalist and cultural critic Margaret Fuller, who had edited the important literary magazine *The Dial* and now wrote for the *New York Daily Tribune*. Eight years Child's junior, Fuller had long looked up to Child as a model of how to be a woman writer. Now that Fuller had a national reputation of her own, the two women came together as peers. They read and commented on each other's work, attended plays and concerts together, and enjoyed long conversations when Fuller, who lived on the outskirts of the city, stayed with Child overnight.

John Hopper, the son of the Quaker couple with whom Child boarded, was an even more intimate friend. They spent many long evenings together, and Hopper often accompanied Child when she explored the city. There were few places the intrepid pair would not go, and in Hopper's company Child went to—and then wrote about—many areas that would have been dangerous for a woman alone. Hopper was 13 years younger than Child, and she often referred to him as her son, but it was obvious that her feelings were more than maternal. "I have come to be *afraid* to lean upon David in all matters connected with a *home* and *support*," she explained to Ellis Loring. "I am weary of moving about; and

FLOWERS FOR CHILDREN.

BY

L. MARIA CHILD,

AUTHOR OF THE MOTHER'S BOOK ; NEW-YORK LETTERS, ETC.

II.

FOR CHILDREN FROM FOUR TO SIX YEARS OLD.

Of all my things I like it best.
Peep in and take a look!
'T is prettier than all the rest,
My little story book.

NEW-YORK:
C. S. FRANCIS & CO., 252 BROADWAY.
BOSTON:
J. H. FRANCIS, 128 WASHINGTON STREET.
1845.

Many of Child's books published during these years were collections of stories and verses for children. These collections never gained the public notice of some of her works for adults, but they brought in a more-or-less steady income that allowed Child to enjoy living in New York City.

John is such a good hand to lean upon...my affections have got so entwined around him, that it would almost kill me to have to leave him. I do hope things will so happen that David and he and I can live together, and bless each other."

Clearly, Child was reconsidering her views of marriage and relations between men and women. For years she had promoted racial equality but shied away from taking a stand for gender equality. Back in 1835, when she published a *History of the Condition of Women,* she amassed an enormous amount of information about women's lives in a vast range of times and places, but she refrained from drawing any conclusions from her data. Later women would use her research to question women's roles in 19th-century America, but Child did not. She summarized her feelings well in an early editorial for the *Standard:* "If I must, at the bidding of conscience, enter the arena and struggle for human rights, I prefer they should be the rights of others, rather than my own."

In two of her final "Letters From New-York," however, Child finally let herself fight for her own rights. She denounced the interwoven ways in which men hold power over women—methods ranging from physical force, to verbal ridicule, to false courtesy (which Child called "taking away *rights,* and *condescending* to grant *privileges*"), to intellectual disparagement. "There are few books which I can read through," she explained, "without feeling insulted as a woman." Take Ralph Waldo Emerson, for example. He told men to "*be, rather than seem*" so that they would "grow up into the full stature of spiritual manhood," but he told women to "*be, rather than seem*" in order to "*gain hearts*" and be "more *pleasing*" to men. The purpose of women's lives, Child protested, was not just to please men. The main problem with the current system, she argued, was men's willingness to use physical force against women: "Whosoever doubts it, let her reflect why she is afraid to go out in the evening without the protection of a man."

In the following years, much of Child's new advocacy for women centered around issues of sexuality, romance, and marriage. Her short stories often featured forbidden love affairs (black and white, Indian and white, or Jew and Greek), failed marriages, or women seeking romantic fulfillment in unconventional ways. In real life, she championed Amelia Norman, a young working woman who was jailed after she tried to murder the "gentleman" who seduced and abandoned her. Child helped turn public opinion in Norman's favor, arguing that men should not be allowed to continue their lives untouched while the women they "ruined" faced disgrace and a choice between starvation and prostitution. When Norman was acquitted, Child took her home, helped her regain her health and spirits, and then found her a job with a New England family. She also helped several other "fallen women" restore their lives. When Margaret Fuller published her *Woman in the Nineteenth Century*—which many male reviewers scorned as indelicate—Child rushed her own favorable reviews into print. "More and more earnestly," she insisted, "rise the questions, '*Is* love a mockery, and marriage a sham? What is woman's true mission? What is the harmonious relation of the sexes?'"

Child had yet to answer these questions in her own life, but the productivity of her New York years suggests that for once her troubles were stimulating rather than draining. Surrounded by friends and music, she had enough happiness to write and many topics to write about.

This halcyon time was not to last. In March 1847, John Hopper eloped with his fiancée. Child wrote that the news "came upon me like a thunderclap" and immediately moved out of the Hopper home. She felt that she could not live under the same roof with John and his wife: she could not watch their happiness while she mourned the loss of her intimacy with John and struggled to subdue her longing for domestic coziness. As soon as she could, she returned to the Carpenters' home in New Rochelle, 30 miles outside of New York City.

This rural location was not conducive to Child's work. She no longer had easy access to New York publishers, and she missed the music and art and conversation that had nourished her imagination. Furthermore, she had taken on a new research project—a history of religious ideas—and the libraries she needed were all back in New York. Every few months she would undertake the long trip into the city to borrow books, but her research now felt like an ordeal.

Isolated and lonely, Child sank into the deepest depression of her life. She recurrently dreamed of death and felt

Margaret Fuller, the most highly educated and intellectual American woman of her time, was a prolific writer, literary critic, and journalist. Her columns written from the battlefields of the 1848 Italian Revolution inspired readers of the New York Daily Tribune.

that she was "all alone on a rock in the middle of the ocean." Although she was only 47, she put her affairs in order and burned more than 300 letters that she thought might be "compromising" if they were found after she died. Life, she frequently wrote, had no more interest for her.

Finally, Child decided to rejoin David. She asked Ellis Loring to buy a small farm in West Newton, Massachusetts, which she and David rented. Child had always hated farm life, but she thought David would benefit from a stable home and hoped they would be able to support themselves if they grew much of their own food. "I want to act with reference to David's good, more than my own," she explained to Loring. Another letter made it clear that David's good was not necessarily her own: "In resigning myself to this inevitable destiny, and conforming my own tastes and inclinations to his, I find peace of mind; but it takes all the electricity out of me." Yet, she also commented, David "is as good as he can be—a nobler, better heart man never had." Child still admired David's moral purity, even though she now under-stood that most of his actions would come to naught.

Three years later, the Childs moved to nearby Wayland so that Child could care for her father, who was now 87 years old, sick and feeble, but as crotchety as ever. For the next three years she stayed by her father's side as he became more and more debilitated. When he died, he left her the small house they had lived in, four acres of land covered with trees suitable for firewood, and $3,200. Finally freed from her nursing duties, Child considered moving into Boston, where she could see her friends and enjoy concerts, lectures, and art exhibitions. David, however, wanted the outdoor exercise of farm life, and Child felt that she could not afford city rents, so they remained in Wayland.

During these years Child finished her history of reli-gious ideas and wrote a biography of John Hopper's father, Isaac, a Quaker philanthropist who helped many fugitive slaves. Otherwise, however, her creativity seemed to disap-pear. "I work hard," she told Loring, "and practise a degree of economy which pinches my soul until I despise its small-ness. Even if I had *time* to write, all power of thinking, and still more of imagining, is pressed out of me by this perpetual load of anxiety." Obsessed with making ends meet, dragging crops out of stony New England soil, keeping David out of trouble, and caring for her father's endless needs, Child felt her horizons narrow to the boundaries of her fields.

Pro-slavery and antislavery settlers converged on Kansas in the 1850s, and both sides were armed by supporters back home. A pro-slavery mob leveled Lawrence, Kansas, in May 1856, and a few months later abolitionists used a picture of the burning Free State Hotel in Lawrence to sell sheet music for a militant antislavery song.

5

A Storm Gathers

The press of historical events did not allow Child to remain forever in her personal doldrums. In 1850, Congress passed the Fugitive Slave Law, which compelled all Northerners to help return escaped slaves or risk criminal prosecution. The law also denied alleged fugitives the right to a jury trial and instead appointed special commissioners who were paid $10 for each person they sent "back" to slavery but only $5 for each person they let go free. Like many other Northerners, Child felt that the new law impinged on her freedom of conscience and put every black person, born free as well as slave, at risk of abduction.

Four years later, the Kansas-Nebraska Act effectively repealed the hard-won Missouri Compromise of 1820 that had brought both Missouri and Maine into the Union. Although the Missouri Compromise had banned slavery from the lands that would become Kansas and Nebraska, the new act allowed residents to vote for themselves whether to allow slavery. Pro-slavery and antislavery settlers rushed to Kansas in order to establish a majority for their side, while Missourians flooded over the border at election time. In Kansas's first election, twice as many people voted as were registered to vote; in one polling place only 20 of more than 600 voters were legal residents. When the fraudulently elected legislature made Kansas a slave state, antislavery settlers established their own, competing, government. Violence frequently broke out at the polls and elsewhere. On May 21, 1856, pro-slavery vigilantes destroyed the antislavery town of Lawrence, Kansas, burning its homes and hotel and smashing its printing press.

Many Northerners were appalled at the news from "Bleeding Kansas." They sent food, clothing, farm implements, and guns to the antislavery settlers. Southerners sent similar aid to the pro-slavery settlers. The Civil War would not officially begin for another five years, but the chasm between North and South turned deadly when Kansans began to shoot at each other.

Events in Washington, D.C., widened that gap. On May 20, the day before Lawrence burned, Senator Charles Sumner of Massachusetts gave a fiery speech denouncing the pro-slavery "ruffians" in Kansas and their Southern supporters, especially Senator Andrew Butler of South Carolina. Two days later, Butler's nephew, the South Carolina congressman Preston Brooks, avenged his uncle's honor. After the Senate adjourned, he approached Sumner, told him that his speech was "a libel on South Carolina and Mr. Butler," and proceeded to beat him over the head with a heavy, gold-tipped cane. More than 30 blows landed while Sumner struggled to get up from his desk. Finally, he collapsed unconscious in a pool of blood.

Far away in Wayland, Child felt both helpless and responsible for Sumner's plight. He credited her *Appeal* with bringing him to the abolitionist cause, and they had become personal friends as well. She longed to rush to Sumner's side and nurse his injuries, but her father was dying and she felt she could not leave. For three days she suffered both physical illness and emotional despair as she thought of Sumner and mourned for her country.

Wayland 21st Dec. 1856

Dearly Beloved Mate,

      The nest has been very cold since you left it. I did bring the cot-bed into the little parlor, and lucky it was that I did it, for I think that first night was as cold as any night we had last winter. The water-pail in the closet was frozen several inches, and the mug of water by my bed-side, though close to the stove, was frozen so hard that I could not break the ice with my hand. The windows were so thickly coated all the following day, that I could not see out of them. All the door-latches were glittering with frost, and my poor plants were all black and drooping. When I kindled a fire in the morning, what should the chimney do but to take fire! It needed burning, and I should have been glad of it, if there had not have been a raging wind. I felt some anxiety, I assure you. I said to myself, "Must I have still another lesson concerning the uncertainty of human affairs? Now that I have, for the first time, the roof-tree so long desired, must it forthwith burn down over my poor old head?" The chimney roared, and the soot fell, for a long time, and when I went out to watch the roof the keen morning blast stung me like fire. Oh, how I wanted my mate! My kind, loving, helpful mate! I felt of the walls and fire-board, up stairs and down stairs, fifty times that day. At last, all became cold; cold enough, I assure you, and here we are, all safe, thank God!

David was in many ways a weak reed, but Child always missed him when he was absent, as this letter to her "Beloved Mate" testifies. Despite her aching loneliness, Child once again proved her ability to cope with events by herself.

Finally, Child determined to lift herself out of her miseries and rededicate herself to eradicating the evil of slavery. She quickly wrote a story, titled "The Kansas Emigrants," that was serialized in the *New York Tribune*. Widely read and discussed, this powerful story helped galvanize Northerners to support the settlers and, more generally, oppose what Child called the "slave power" of the South.

In 1859 the violence reached Virginia. John Brown, a white Northerner who had fought in Kansas, led a group of 21 men, both black and white, in an assault on the federal arsenal in Harpers Ferry. He hoped the attack would provoke a general uprising of slaves, who would then use the arsenal's weapons to free more and more plantations. The group easily captured the arsenal, but the next morning it was recaptured by federal troops. Ten men, including both of Brown's sons, were killed, and Brown was stabbed with a sword after he agreed to surrender.

The whole country erupted with controversy over Brown's actions. Many people—even many abolitionists—abhorred his use of violence. Others saw him as a martyr, especially after he was convicted of murder, treason, and conspiracy to foment slave insurrection and sentenced to hang. Despite Child's pacifist tendencies, she admired Brown's courage and willingness to risk his life for the slaves. She immediately wrote to Brown, offering to go to Virginia and nurse him. "Believing in peace principles," she told him, "I cannot sympathize with the method you chose to advance the cause of freedom. But I honor your generous intentions, I admire your courage, moral and physical, I reverence you for the humanity which tempered your zeal, I sympathize with your cruel bereavements, your sufferings, and your wrongs."

The governor of Virginia, Henry Wise, was Brown's official guardian, so Child sent her letter to him along with a request for permission to nurse Brown. Wise wrote back a disapproving letter in which he guaranteed her safety if she came to Virginia but also accused her of creating the moral atmosphere that led to Brown's assault. "His attempt," Wise claimed, "was a natural consequence of your sympathy."

Thinking that he had written an effective rebuke, Wise sent both his and Child's letters to a variety of newspapers. Child responded by publishing an "Explanatory Letter" and a letter she had received from Brown himself. Then Margaretta Mason, the wife of Virginia's Senator James Mason, wrote a public letter in which she accused Child of hypocrisy and selfishness. Abolitionists, Mason declared, ignore the needs of their own neighbors and do not really care about anyone. Child's 11-page response—also published—systematically revealed Mason's ignorance and faulty logic. After Northerners help a woman in childbirth, Child's letter concluded, *we do not sell the babies.*"

This flurry of letters reestablished Child's place at the forefront of the abolitionist movement. Because Wise and Mason sent their letters to Southern newspapers, Child's ideas finally made it into the Southern press that had frozen her out for almost 30 years. The American Anti-Slavery Society gathered all of the correspondence into a pamphlet and distributed 300,000 copies throughout the free states— an enormous coverage in a time when there were only 20 million people outside the South. The letters represented Brown and his men as levelheaded and sympathetic martyrs and did much to rally Northern opinion behind Brown.

Brown politely refused Child's offer to nurse him, but instead asked her to create a "little fund" for the support of his wife and young children and his sons' widows and children. Child promptly set to work raising money for the fund but expanded Brown's request to include all of the Harpers Ferry group, "especially the *colored* men." She was dismayed when Brown's followers were sentenced to hang. "Those poor *young* victims were not so raised above their fate, as their leader was," she wrote to friends. "They wanted to *live;* & my heart ached for them."

Throughout this time, Child continued to counsel non-violence because she believed violence is always wrong. But in a public letter to William Lloyd Garrison, she suggested that violence might prove inevitable. "If I believed our religion justified men in fighting for freedom," she told Governor Wise, "I should consider the enslaved everywhere as best entitled to that right." Referring to the heroes of the American Revolution, she suggested that Harpers Ferry was "the 'Concord *Fight*' of an impending revolution."

The abolitionists had failed to eradicate slavery by peaceful means, so abolition would come by violent means, "because come it *must*." Only people who condemned war "under *any* circumstances," she insisted, could criticize Brown. Anyone else—anyone who praised the American Revolution—must see that Brown's cause was just and right. "It is very inconsistent," she argued in Garrison's abolitionist newspaper, the *Liberator,* "to eulogize Lafayette for volunteering to aid in *our* fight for freedom, while we blame John Brown for going to the rescue of those who are a thousand times more oppressed than we ever were, and who have none to help them."

The Virginia courts did not agree, and John Brown was hanged on December 2, 1859. Throughout the country, abolitionists marked the day with special church services and other solemn observances. Child attended a day-long prayer meeting at a black church before joining Garrison for a large evening commemoration in downtown Boston. She appreciated black Bostonians' unambivalent embrace of Brown, but she mourned the rising tide of violence.

Child sometimes feared that war was inevitable, but she hoped it could be averted. The North, she argued in letters to newspapers, should peacefully disentangle itself from slavery by seceding from the South. Without Northerners' support, she predicted, the slave system would become unsustainable. Slaves would know that safety was just on the other side of the Northern border, so many more of them

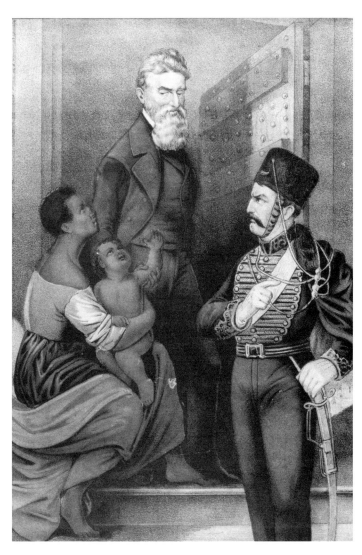

A legend quickly spread that John Brown had stopped to kiss a black child on his way to the gallows. This popular print conveyed the widespread feeling that tenderness and goodwill underlay his violent deeds. Such portrayals helped many people, even pacifists such as Child, see him as a martyr.

would flee their oppressors. Without federal troops Southern whites would have less power to suppress slave insurrections, so a real revolution might occur. Meanwhile, the North could finally become a true republic with liberty and justice for all.

The idea of Northern secession did not capture the public's imagination, so Child sought other ways to prevent war. Her new pamphlet, titled *The Right Way the Safe Way*, tried to convince Southerners to free their slaves voluntarily. In it, Child detailed the results of emancipation in the British West Indies and briefly touched upon the experiences of the French West Indies, South Africa, Mexico, South America, Java, and the Swedish and Danish colonies—all of which had peacefully emancipated slaves. She let her sources speak for themselves, with no additional moralizing, as she presented a "*business*-view" of slavery and emancipation. Emancipation, she concluded, produced temporary inconvenience but long-term prosperity, whereas slavery led to economic stagnation and violent slave insurrections.

Child personally sent more than a thousand copies of *The Right Way the Safe Way* to congressmen, governors, judges, and ordinary Southerners whose addresses she had been able to locate. The pamphlet was especially influential in the western part of Virginia, where the soil was too poor for plantation agriculture and the local economy therefore did not depend much on slavery. When Virginia seceded from the Union, its western counties seceded from the rest of the state and created the state of West Virginia, which rejoined the Union and emancipated its slaves.

Child's new pamphlet aimed at Northerners—*The Patriarchal Institution, as Described by Members of Its Own Family*—was far more inflammatory. Pro-slavery writers often claimed that slaves were better off than Northern wage workers, who in an age before Social Security and welfare programs had no protection against illness, accidents, unemployment, or poverty in old age. Employers could fire workers at will, Southerners argued, while slave owners had to feed and shelter their slaves whether or not they could work.

Child used Southerners' own words to provide, as she put it, a "very sarcastic" portrait of slave owners' benevolence— a benevolence that had to be enforced with horsewhips and chains. The slave owners' real goal, she warned Northern white workers, was to reduce all working people to slavery. She quoted a Southern writer: "*Slavery is the natural and normal condition of the laboring man, white or black.*" Unless white

EMANCIPATION NEVER LEADS TO BLOODSHED

These excerpts from The Right Way the Safe Way *(1860) illustrate Child's use of economic data and historical events to argue for abolition on purely practical, not moral, grounds. She hoped that slaveholders would voluntarily free their slaves—and thus forestall the Civil War—if they realized that emancipation would increase their wealth and physical security.*

In Mauritius, a fertile island in the Indian Ocean, belonging to Great Britain, the sugar crop, during the last ten years of slavery, averaged 68,741,120 lbs. annually. During four years, after emancipation, beginning with 1845, the average crop was 171,122,500 lbs.; an increase of 102 millions of pounds annually; nearly 150 per cent in favor of free labor. . . .

Whenever immediate emancipation is urged, the "horrors of St. Domingo [Haiti]" are always brought forward to prove it dangerous. This is one of numerous misstatements originating in prejudice, and afterward taken for granted by those who have not examined the subject. The first troubles between the white and black races in St. Domingo were the result of oppressive and unlawful treatment of the free colored population. . . . The next troubles were occasioned by an attempt to *restore slavery*, after it had been for some years abolished. It was never the *granting* of rights to the colored people that produced bloodshed or disturbance. All the disasters to the whites came in consequence of *withholding* those rights. . . .

History proves that emancipation has always been safe. It is an undeniable fact, that not one white person has ever been killed, or wounded, or had life or property endangered by any violence attendant upon immediate emancipation, in any of the many cases where the experiment has been tried.

workers learned to see black men and women as their compatriots, and rescued them from the tyranny of slavery, Child concluded, their own children might end up in chains as well.

The Patriarchal Institution and Child's numerous newspaper articles both reflected and reinforced Northerners' anger at the South. Many Northerners felt that they had made one compromise after another, only to find that 40 years of compromise had increased Southerners' demands and the power of the slave system. The time for compromise and concession, Child now insisted, was over. North and South were fundamentally and morally divided, and the North must no longer subordinate its republican ideals to the slave power. Such heated rhetoric fueled Northerners' determination to stand up to the South.

Child also found time to edit an autobiography written by Harriet Jacobs, an escaped slave from North Carolina. For seven years Jacobs hid above the ceiling of her grandmother's cabin, in a small cavity where she could never stand up, before she finally found an opportunity to flee to the North. Several years later a publisher agreed to print her story if Child would write a preface for it. Jacobs approached Child with trepidation, but Child was glad to help and the two women became close friends. *Incidents in the Life of a Slave Girl* would become one of the most frequently read slave narratives. Its vivid descriptions of sexual harassment underlined the vulnerability of slave women—and slave girls— to their white masters.

Like many owners of fugitive slaves, Harriet Jacobs's master offered an award for her return and threatened to prosecute anyone who aided her. Jacobs's master claimed she had no "cause or provocation" for leaving. In fact, he was jealous of her children's father and furious at her refusal to become his mistress.

$100 REWARD

WILL be given for the apprehension and delivery of my Servant Girl HARRIET. She is a light mulatto, 21 years of age, about 5 feet 4 inches high, of a thick and corpulent habit, having on her head a thick covering of black hair that curls naturally, but which can be easily combed straight. She speaks easily and fluently, and has an agreeable carriage and address. Being a good seamstress, she has been accustomed to dress well, has a variety of very fine clothes, made in the prevailing fashion, and will probably appear, if abroad, tricked out in gay and fashionable finery. As this girl absconded from the plantation of my son without any known cause or provocation, it is probable she designs to transport herself to the North.

The above reward, with all reasonable charges, will be given for apprehending her, or securing her in any prison or jail within the U. States.

All persons are hereby forewarned against harboring or entertaining her, or being in any way instrumental in her escape, under the most rigorous penalties of the law.

These writings once again made Child a significant public fugure. Even though she remained in Wayland, and rarely ventured even into Boston, she helped form public opinion throughout the North. She held no position of power or authority. Instead, she had influence: an indirect power that enabled her to help shape the most decisive events of her time.

Child delighted in her renewed sense of purpose as she watched Northerners finally come around to the abolitionist beliefs she had embraced 30 years earlier. After all those years of frustration and failure, she could see that both her past and her present actions had real effects. "When there is anti-slavery work to be done, I feel as young as twenty," she wrote to the Quaker abolitionist and women's rights leader Lucretia Mott. "When Anthony Burns [a fugitive slave] was carried from Boston, and when Charles Sumner was stricken down in the Senate, I swore a solemn oath, in the depths of my soul, that, so long as God spared my life, I would hunt the Demon Slavery with all the energy and all the activity I possessed." No longer plagued by energy-sapping depression, Child did everything she could to help the antislavery cause.

She also, however, had come to resent the limitations placed on her because she was female. "At times," she wrote to Sumner, "my old heart swells almost to bursting, in view of all these things; for it is the heart of a man imprisoned within a woman's destiny." Child could have influence—the indirect power of the pen—but she could not vote, run for office, or otherwise directly participate in the mounting tide of events. When Northampton raised the taxes on a farm David owned there, Child exploded in fury to Ellis Loring: "I mean to petition the Legislature to exempt me from taxes, or grant me the privilege of *voting*. Oh *what* a sex you are! It's time you were turned out of office. *High* time. You've been captains long enough. It's *our* turn now."

Back in the 1830s, Child had argued that political power was not as important as public opinion: the only way

John Frémont's Presidential campaign banner showed him and his running mate, John Cochrane, surrounded by American flags, an eagle, and a field of stars. The cornucopias suggested that Republican leadership would yield economic prosperity.

to really change people, she believed, was to change their thinking, not to pass laws. Because she considered politics ineffective, she did not care that women were excluded from it. As she grew older, however, and as the country began to move toward war, she realized that politics could be important. She therefore protested women's exclusion from decisions that affected everyone.

The election of 1856, Child felt, was especially critical. The Republican party—a coalition of abolitionists and of "Free Soil" men who wanted to exclude blacks from immigrating to the new territories—had been organized in

1854. Their first Presidential candidate, John Frémont, ran in 1856 with a promise to prevent the expansion of slavery. Child was inspired by the thought of having such a man in the White House—and even more inspired by his articulate and charismatic wife, Jessie Frémont. She wrote to her friend Sarah Shaw:

> What a shame that *women* can't vote! We'd carry "our Jessie" into the White House on our shoulders; *would*n't we?... I never was bitten by politics before; but such mighty issues are depending on *this* election, that I cannot be indifferent. Backward or forward the car of human freedom must roll. It cannot stand still.

Child had always believed that women should be able to do anything that helped the human race. Now she believed that they should be able to vote.

Although Frémont lost the election to the Southern sympathizer James Buchanan, Child did not give up her interest in politics. In fact, it even improved her relationship with David. Long before they met, David had a passion for politics. Indeed, his political interests fueled Child's disinterest: all she saw coming from the *Massachusetts Journal* and David's other political forays were debt, lawsuits, and broken friendships. No wonder she was willing to leave the "snare" of politics to the men. When Kansas erupted, however, politics became a joint interest. David could be a political actor in ways that Child could not: he could vote, and he could also attend political meetings and travel on behalf of the Kansas Aid Committee. The two of them were finally able to complement each other and work toward a common goal.

In other ways, as well, the Childs' marriage became more peaceful. David no longer spent Child's money thoughtlessly, coming home to announce some new purchase that broke her already-strained budget. Instead, he let Child make all the financial decisions and praised her "industry, frugality, & generosity." Finances were less tight after they moved in with Child's father, because they did not have to pay rent, and Child's modest inheritance also helped. When David received a small inheritance from his uncle, he offered to contribute the interest to household expenses. Child refused his offer. "I told him," she later wrote to his sister, "I wanted him to keep it for his own especial use; to buy books, or maps, or any superfluity he took a fancy to; and he did so. Though the dear, generous, kind soul was always *offering* it to me." Child, it seems, had accepted full financial responsibility for the family and no longer expected any contribution from David.

Meanwhile, the tide of events continued to move the country toward war. Child was delighted when the Republican candidate, Abraham Lincoln, won the Presidential

The exterior of Fort Sumter showed significant damage on April 14, 1861, after federal troops had surrendered to the Confederates and evacuated the fort. During the next four years, 618,000 Americans would die in the Civil War and 550,000 more would be permanently maimed.

election in 1860. A month later South Carolina seceded from the Union and other Southern states followed its example. Many Northern businessmen and workers feared that secession or war would bring economic ruin, so they pressured the government to appease the Southern states. Congress even passed a constitutional amendment guaranteeing that the federal government would never interfere with states' laws regarding slavery—though the war started so soon afterward that the amendment did not have time to go to the states for ratification. Anti-abolitionist riots broke out across the North, and abolitionists feared for their lives almost as much as they had during the "mob year" of 1835. Once again Child used her privileged status as a woman—whom most men would not attack—to smuggle abolitionist speakers through irate crowds.

Northerners remained fractured until the Confederates began to shell Fort Sumter on April 12, 1861. The federal fort was located in the harbor of Charleston, South Carolina, and the state had not allowed it to receive food or other supplies since December. The hungry soldiers soon surrendered, and the next day Lincoln called for 75,000 militiamen to put down the "insurrection." The Civil War had begun.

ABE LINCOLN'S LAST CARD; OR, ROUGE-ET-NOIR.

This cartoon implies that Lincoln saw the abolition of slavery as a tactic, not a goal, in a deadly game of cards between North and South. Lincoln's expression suggests that he was none too happy to play the emancipation card, but the confident smile on the Southerner's face suggests that he saw Lincoln's move for what it was: an act of desperation.

6

WAR AND
ITS AFTERMATH

Child's pacifist principles made it very difficult for her to support any war. Furthermore, her goals were very different from Abraham Lincoln's. When the war began, Lincoln intended to restore the Union, not to eradicate slavery. Like most Northerners, he believed that slave owners' property rights were guaranteed by the Constitution. He also did not want to alienate the slave states—Delaware, Maryland, and Kentucky—that had remained in the Union. "If I could save the Union without freeing *any* slave, I would do it," he explained to Horace Greeley of the *New York Daily Tribune.* "If I could save it by freeing *all* the slaves, I would do it; and if I could do it by freeing some and leaving others alone, I would also do that. What I do about Slavery and the colored race, I do because I believe it helps to save this Union."

Child, in contrast, had argued for years that the North should secede from the Union, so she was appalled by the prospect of a war just to save the Union. She hoped war would somehow lead to abolition, but feared it would not. Perhaps her greatest fear was that the war would end too soon, the South would return to the Union, and nothing else would change. If slavery survived, she felt, all the suffering and death of war would be for nothing.

Many slaves took the question of freedom into their own hands: they fled their owners and sought refuge in Union army camps. At first, military officers did not welcome the fugitives and often helped return them to their owners. Child was furious when 30 Florida slaves who offered to work for the Union were sent back to their masters in chains. "God knows I *want* to love and honor the flag of my country," she wrote, "but how *can* I, when it is used for *such* purposes?" When she was given a patriotic pin in the form of an American flag, she rejected it indignantly. "I would as soon wear the rattlesnake upon my bosom as the eagle," she told her friend Sarah Shaw.

As she had so many times before, Child wrote to the newspapers to try to convert others to her perspective. The Union, she insisted, should serve both its own interests and the cause of justice by protecting fugitive slaves and putting them to work. Held captive on Southern plantations, slaves involuntarily helped the Confederate cause by growing food and cotton, supplying their masters' needs, and generating profits that could be used to buy ammunition and other war materials. Rebels, Child argued, forfeited their constitutional rights by engaging in treason. If they ever had a property right to slaves, that right evaporated when they took up arms against their country. The army should therefore shelter fugitives and find ways to use their willing labor to help the Union, rather than send them back to help the Confederacy.

As the self-emancipated slaves continued to flood into Union camps, Lincoln eventually declared them "contraband of war": valuable resources that could strengthen either side and should therefore be kept from the rebels. John Frémont, now the Union commander in charge of the Missouri campaign, took this principle to the next logical step. Missourian rebels, he proclaimed, forfeited all their property rights, including their right to hold slaves. Lincoln was not ready for such broad emancipation, so he quickly revoked Frémont's order. Child fumed that no one, except the abolitionists, seemed even to consider justice for the fugitives. "*They* are *property*," she wrote sarcastically, "to be disposed of in *any* way, according as the laws of war, or the patching up of the Union, may seem to render expedient."

In addition to her political agitation, Child tried to help the fugitives directly. Most "contraband" had no way to earn wages, since the army refused to hire them until the later stages of the war, and they needed warm clothing and bedding as winter settled in. Child coordinated relief efforts and personally sent blankets, warm hats, secondhand clothing, and sewing and knitting supplies to the refugee camps so the former slaves could make things for themselves. She also sent easy books, so they might learn to read, and copies of her antislavery writings. She wanted not just to provide for the fugitives' physical needs—urgent though they were—but also to help them prepare for freedom.

As the months went by, it became clear that neither North nor South would have a quick victory. In an open letter to President Lincoln, which was widely published in Northern newspapers, Child chastised him for delaying emancipation. The American people, she wrote, were willing to "sacrifice their fortunes and their lives," but they "very reasonably wish to know what they are sacrificing them for." Only "great ideas of Justice and Freedom," she insisted, could sustain people through a lengthy war.

Child could not know that Lincoln had already decided to emancipate the slaves but was waiting for a military victory so that the announcement would seem like a sign of strength rather than weakness. Finally, after a long series of Union defeats, Union forces prevented the Confederate troops from invading Maryland, and Lincoln released his Emancipation Proclamation. Child was pleased by this proclamation but not completely satisfied. Emancipation was announced in September but did not go into effect until January, and Child worried about what might happen during those three months. She was also angry that Lincoln still represented emancipation purely as "a war measure," with no "principles of justice or humanity" behind it. Nevertheless, the proclamation meant that—if the Union won the war—all slaves in rebel states would eventually be freed. Child took satisfaction in that partial fulfillment of her dream.

The final version of the Emancipation Proclamation, released on January 1, 1863, was more idealistic and therefore more to Child's taste. The proclamation declared itself "an act of justice, warranted by the Constitution." It also specifically stated that freed slaves would be welcomed into the Union army. No longer would only whites be allowed to fight for the Union—a divisive policy that Child had often protested. With these two changes, Child could finally support the Union cause. She regretted the suffering and death associated with war, but felt they were an acceptable price for eliminating the even greater suffering and death associated with slavery.

The Union army soon accepted its first regiment of former slaves, the First South Carolina Volunteers. Shortly thereafter, Massachusetts created two regiments of free blacks, one of which was headed by Robert Gould Shaw, the son of Child's close friends Sarah and Francis Shaw. Child was delighted by Robert's glowing reports of the men under his command, which confirmed her long-standing belief that blacks were capable of just as much achievement and heroism as whites.

Her aspirations were both confirmed and dashed when Shaw's 54th Massachusetts Regiment was assigned the suicidal mission of attacking Fort Wagner, which guarded Charleston, South Carolina. His men had to approach the fort along an open beach, which made them easy targets for Confederate guns, cannons, and hand grenades. Almost half of the regiment's soldiers were killed, wounded, or captured. Shaw

himself was killed and then stripped of his uniform, watch, and antique ring and thrown into a mass grave with his soldiers. The Confederates considered this one of the worst insults that could be given to a white man, but his abolitionist parents informed the public that Shaw had "received at the hands of the rebels the most fitting burial possible—with his brave, devoted followers." Child felt enormous sympathy for her friends at the loss of their promising son, whom she had known since he was a boy. She was even more dismayed by the fate of the captured soldiers, who were reportedly sold as slaves. For two days she was incapacitated by grief.

At roughly the same time, Child learned that New York City had erupted in the largest riot of the 19th century. The Union had instituted an involuntary draft in order to keep up its fighting forces in the face of heavy losses, but the law exempted any man who could give the army $300—a year's wages for an unskilled laborer. Working-class

One of the largest crowds in Boston's history gathered to cheer Child's friend Robert Gould Shaw and the soldiers of the black 54th Massachusetts Regiment as they left the city on May 28, 1863. This memorial in Boston portrays Shaw moving in solidarity with his men as an angel above guides them all to freedom.

white protesters first burned down a conscription station (where drafted men were prepared for induction into the army), then attacked well-dressed and presumably wealthy men, then turned on black people. Blacks, they claimed, had caused the war—even though most of the blacks in New York had been free for generations. Any black man or boy unlucky enough to be on the streets was quickly surrounded by hundreds of rioters. Crowds dragged black men out of their homes and lynched them on the city's trees and lampposts, set fire to black people's houses, and looted and burned the Colored Orphan Asylum. More than a hundred people died in the violence.

These events reinforced Child's determination to define the Civil War as a war not just against slavery but against racism. Some abolitionists—including William Lloyd Garrison—believed their work would be done when the slaves were emancipated. Child, however, believed that justice would not be served until black people were fully equal members of American society. The freed slaves, she recognized, would need education, paid work, and equal protection of the laws. None of these could be taken for granted.

Still, there were many signs of progress. Union soldiers who saw slavery for themselves, and then fought beside black soldiers in battle, often returned home with transformed attitudes. One of the Childs' neighbors, a naval captain, had suggested that they should be "mobbed" when they argued that the slaves should be freed and given weapons to fight in the Union army. Now he came home and publicly announced that his opinions of blacks had changed. When a passenger in a streetcar insulted a black soldier and refused to sit near him, the captain stood up in his uniform and said, "Come here, my good fellow! I've been fighting along side people of your color, and glad enough I was to *have* 'em by my side. Come and sit by *me*." Child was heartened by such indications that American racism was finally weakening.

As the war neared its end, and a Union victory seemed likely, Child gained something of the status of a senior stateswoman. As she had predicted, many Northerners felt that only some great good—such as emancipation—could justify the many lives lost or ruined by the war. They therefore rallied around the goal of emancipation, even if just a few years earlier they had been opposed or indifferent to it. For 35 years Child had lobbied for abolition, and many people now praised her foresightedness. Newspapers vied for her writings and she was considered one of the most influential shapers of Northern public opinion.

Like most Northerners, Child was horrified when Lincoln was killed by an assassin's bullet on April 14, 1865 —only five days after the Confederate general Robert E. Lee surrendered at the Appomattox Court House. Privately, however, she wondered whether some act of Providence might underlie the tragic event. Perhaps, she thought, Lincoln's Vice President, Andrew Johnson—a Southern "poor white"—would be a better leader as the country sought to heal its wounds. Because he had one foot in each world, he might be able to bridge regional and class antagonisms and create a more equal and just society. She was to be sorely disappointed.

Even before the war ended, Child had begun to plan for the future economic development of the South. Southern agriculture, industry, and transportation routes were devastated by the war, which was mostly fought on Southern soil. If the whole South were reduced to poverty, Child predicted, the freed slaves would not have opportunities to improve their

"Let the stain of innocent blood be removed from the land by the arrest and punishment of the murderers," pleaded this broadside, which was distributed immediately after Lincoln was shot. In a country so recently torn by civil war, many people feared that the nation would fall into chaos without its wartime leader.

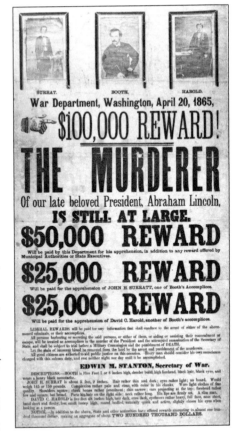

lives and racial tensions would increase. Economic redevelopment was therefore essential for racial justice.

The Union, Child argued, should confiscate large plantations owned by rebels, break them down into smaller lots, and sell them at modest prices to former slaves, former soldiers (black or white), and European immigrants. Such small farms, she explained, would allow the South to rebuild its agricultural system without the large plantations that required slaves or other workers who could be paid subsistence wages or less. Some abolitionists argued that former slaves should receive land for free, because they had worked so long without wages. Child disagreed. People, she believed, would not value land they did not pay for, so it would end up in the hands of speculators or opportunistic immigrants. Better to wait until families had earned a little bit of money and could take pride in their ability to buy property and care for it.

After the war, Child discovered to her frustration that these questions were pointless. Congress restored the property rights of all but a very few Confederate leaders, so almost all of the plantations remained intact. Little land was available for establishing new farms and new ways of life.

Congress was dominated by Republicans, who wanted to give the freedmen political and civil rights (though not land or any other sort of economic compensation for their years of unpaid labor). Johnson, in contrast, wanted to return the country, as much as possible, to its prewar condition. He granted amnesty to most ex-Confederates and even indicated that he would readmit rebel states to the Union with no provisions for black suffrage. When Congress passed a Civil Rights Bill, which defined blacks as U.S. citizens with full rights of citizenship, Johnson vetoed it. Congress overrode the veto, but from then on Congress and the President were pitted against each other. Congress would pass laws over Johnson's veto, but Johnson would refuse to enforce them. His overt sabotage of congressional legislation led to the first impeachment of an American President. (Johnson was acquitted by the Senate after a trial in 1868.)

Child had little influence over these political machinations. She did not have the taste, talent, or expertise to advise legislators about the political strategies necessary to achieve their goals, and she sadly concluded that Johnson had no moral principles to call upon. Ironically, then, just as Child's national reputation reached its peak, the most important struggle for black people's rights centered in a place—Washington, D.C.—where her skills for mobilizing popular opinion were of little use.

Many people, even those who tried not to be racist, opposed giving the vote to former slaves. Southern states had made it a crime to teach slaves to read. Most freed people were therefore illiterate, and many Northerners as well as Southerners feared that they would remain too ignorant to vote responsibly. Child agreed that slavery was poor preparation for republican citizenship, but she argued that slave ownership was even worse preparation because it trained people to disregard other people's basic rights as human beings. If ex-Confederates were allowed to vote, she insisted, ex-slaves should also be allowed to vote—if for no other reason than to protect themselves politically against their former masters.

Furthermore, Child pointed out, many poor whites, especially immigrants, were also illiterate or uneducated, but they had the vote. The only acceptable solution, she concluded, was to educate both blacks and whites as quickly as possible so that they could become informed and responsible citizens.

Child did her part in this enormous endeavor by editing *The Freedmen's Book*. As she explained in its preface, *The Freedmen's Book* was intended not just to teach freed people how to read, but also to prepare them more generally for their future. It included essays about black history; biographies of successful black people; poetry about freedom, hope, and suffering; stories about slaves; and Child's advice about how to create new lives as free people. Several of the contributions were written by blacks, including both famous writers (such as the colonial poet Phillis Wheatley and the abolitionist Frederick Douglass) and obscure former slaves, who might not even have a last name. Child put an asterisk beside the names of all black contributors in order to prove to readers that black people can be effective writers.

The Freedmen's Book candidly described the injustices black people had faced and the oppressive actions of white

Prominent black names from past and present filled the table of contents of Child's Freedmen's Book. After reading this book, no one could imagine that blacks were unintelligent or incompetent.

CONTENTS.

———◆———

* The names of the colored authors are marked with an asterisk.

people around the world, but it also celebrated black people's intelligence, virtue, and dedication to freedom. Child wanted former slaves to know that black people could be educated, accomplished, and influential. Appropriate racial pride, she believed, would help freed people advance themselves without bitter recriminations against their former masters. Education, self-respect, and a combination of independence and cooperation would lead them to full liberty and justice.

Child wanted to sell *The Freedmen's Book* as cheaply as possible, but she also wanted to make it durable and appealing. Unfortunately, she did not have the money for such a project and she could not find a sponsor. Finally, she finished a collection of inspirational stories and essays for the elderly and discovered, to her surprise, that it sold out in only two months. Child used the proceeds from these remarkable sales to publish and distribute her *Freedmen's Book*. Everything she earned she used to print more copies.

Many freed people preferred Child's volume to its primary competitor, *The Freedman's Third Reader,* which was published by the American Tract Society and sought to instill Christian piety and American patriotism. *The Freedmen's Book* encouraged readers to reflect on their experiences and see themselves in a larger context, while the *Third Reader* exhorted them to live up to white, middle-class standards. Child tried her best to make *The Freedmen's Book* available, but her resources were tiny compared to the well-funded Tract Society, so her book was used in relatively few schools. Wherever it appeared, however, it left an impact: many freed people memorized its poems or retold its stories.

Soon Child was facing a new question: what about woman suffrage? The 14th Amendment, which was passed in 1868 and guaranteed citizenship to anyone born or naturalized in the United States, specified that only men had full political rights. This was the first time that the Constitution

text continues on page 102

CHARACTER CAN OVERCOME

Child's introduction to The Freedmen's Book *(1865) listed black men and women whom she considered worthy of emulation. The first four that she mentions below were political, scientific, or literary figures, but William and Ellen Craft were ordinary people who had proven their courage and resourcefulness by escaping from slavery. Ellen, who was light-skinned, pretended to be an ailing white gentleman traveling with a black slave (William) from Georgia to Philadelphia. All people, Child suggested, can demonstrate heroism, however humble their circumstances.*

I have made this book to encourage you to exertion by examples of what colored people are capable of doing. Such men and women as Toussaint l'Ouverture, Benjamin Banneker, Phillis Wheatley, Frederick Douglass, and William and Ellen Craft, prove that the power of *character* can overcome all external disadvantages, even that most crushing of all disadvantages, Slavery. . . .

Perhaps few of you will be able to stir the hearts of large assemblies by such eloquent appeals as those of Frederick Douglass, or be able to describe what you have seen and heard so gracefully as [the author] Charlotte L. Forten does. Probably none of you will be called to govern a state as Toussaint L'Ouverture did; for such a remarkable career as his does not happen once in hundreds of years. . . . [B]ut you have one great opportunity peculiar to yourselves. You can do a vast amount of good to people in various parts of the world, and through the generations, by simply being sober, industrious, and honest. . . . [I]f your houses look neat, and your clothes are clean and whole, and your gardens well weeded, and your work faithfully done, whether for yourselves or others, then all the world will cry out, "You see that negroes *can* take care of themselves; and it is a sin and a shame to keep such men in Slavery." Thus, while you are serving your own interests, you will be helping on the emancipation of poor weary slaves in other parts of the world. . . .

I think it would generally be well for you to work for your former masters, if they treat you well, and pay you as much as you could earn elsewhere. But if they show a disposition to oppress you, quit their service and work for somebody who will treat you like freemen. If they use violent language to you, never use impudent language to them. If they cheat you, scorn to cheat them in return. If they propose to women such connections as used to be common under the bad system of Slavery, teach them that freedwomen not only have the legal power to protect themselves from such degradation, but also that they have pride of character. . . . If you pursue this course you will always be superior, however rich or elegant may be the man or woman who wrongs you.

I do not mean by this that you ought to submit tamely to insult or oppression. Stand up for your rights, but do it in a manly way. Quit working for a man who speaks to you contemptuously, or who tries to take mean advantage of you. . . . If it becomes necessary, apply to magistrates to protect you and redress your wrongs. . . [or write] to some of your firm friends in Congress, such as the Hon. Charles Sumner, the Hon. Henry Wilson, and the Hon. George W. Julian. . . .

The providence of God has opened for you an upward path. Walk ye in it, without being discouraged by the brambles and stones at the outset. Those who come after you will clear them away, and will place in their stead strong, smooth rails for the steam-car called Progress of the Colored Race.

text continued from page 99

explicitly excluded women, and many politically active women therefore opposed the amendment. Other women, however, believed that it was most important for black men to get political power, so that freed people would be able to defend themselves through the law. Woman suffrage, they felt, could be addressed later. Child belonged to the second group. "The suffrage of woman can better afford to wait than that of the colored people," she explained. The most important goal of the decade, she believed, was to empower freed people and prevent the reestablishment of white supremacy in the South.

Nevertheless, Child began to write more frequently about woman suffrage and women's rights. Women and men, she argued, are not much different, and only "conventional prejudices" keep women in a subordinate position. As women become more educated and more active in every aspect of life, she predicted, their presence will become unremarkable— just as unremarkable as the absence of the veil that virtuous women wore in previous centuries. In a letter to Charles Sumner, Child explicitly likened the restrictions of women's lives to the shackles that bound slaves. "For forty years, I have keenly felt the cramping effects of my limitations as a woman," she told him. "I have walked in fetters thus far, and my pilgrimage is drawing to a close."

Before it finally drew to a close, however, Child would renew one of her first crusades: the crusade for Indians' rights. The Civil War had been disastrous for Indians. Both Union and Confederate troops built roads and railways across their lands and forcibly drove them out of their homes. Wars between the Native Americans and the Union government broke out in both 1862 and 1864, and the battles continued after the Civil War ended. Army officers insisted that Indians should be confined to reservations or exterminated altogether. Indians, not surprisingly, wanted to continue to live as their ancestors had. "All who cling to

Publisher Louis Prang honored Child as one of seven "representative women" in this 1870 lithograph. Clockwise from the bottom of the circle are Child, Susan B. Anthony, Grace Greenwood, Lucretia Mott, Elizabeth Cady Stanton, and Mary Livermore; Anna Dickinson is in the center.

their old hunting ground," the Union hero General William T. Sherman declared, "are hostile and will remain so until killed off." The Plains Indians usually broke into small groups for the winter, and army troops began to systematically seek out the winter encampments and exterminate their occupants.

Child's new "Appeal for the Indians," published in the *National Anti-Slavery Standard,* denounced the slaughter of Native Americans, their loss of ancestral lands, and the callous disregard of their civil rights. Abolitionists, she argued, should be just as concerned about crimes against Indians as crimes against blacks. Her goal, as it had been 40 years earlier, was to enable Indians to assimilate peacefully into the dominant American culture. Much of her "Appeal" was a systematic refutation of the "almost universal opinion that Indians are incapable of civilization." If Indians were allowed to hold property, attend school, and even intermarry with whites, she explained, they would eventually become indistinguishable from the mass of Americans. For Indians, as for blacks, she could see no better future. She sometimes suggested that white people could learn something from Indians—especially from their egalitarian treatment of women and children—but for the most part she assumed that Indian culture would disappear through assimilation.

Child's "Appeal" successfully engaged abolitionists in the Indian rights movement and linked them with other Indian rights advocates. The result of their agitation was the Dawes Act of 1887, in which the federal government denied the existence of Indian tribes and announced that it would thereafter deal with Indians only as individuals. Indians would be allowed to hold land as individuals, not as tribes, and any prior agreement or treaty with an Indian tribe was declared void. The goal of the Dawes Act was to destroy Indians' tribal loyalties and inherited customs, settle each family on a small plot of land, and use the lure of private property and U.S. citizenship to force Indians to assimilate into white culture. Child and her like-minded contemporaries thus managed to slow the extermination of Native Americans, but only by legalizing the extermination of Indian culture.

Child's abolitionist work was more successful: after more than 30 years of activism, she had the great satisfaction of seeing slavery abolished throughout the United States. Racism remained strong, however, in both North and South, and Child correctly feared that President Johnson's policies and the lack of economic reconstruction in the South would lead to a resurgence of white supremacy. "When people ask me," she wrote, "if I am not thankful to have lived to see justice done to the negro, I reply, 'If I do live to see justice done him, I shall be thankful.'"

Instead, Child witnessed the rapid deterioration of black people's lives as federal troops pulled out of the South and control of Southern states was returned to their residents. In many states, blacks were all but reenslaved in the 1870s by new laws that limited their freedom to travel and to work. Many had to labor on white-owned plantations for subsistence wages or less. Any black man or woman who could not prove employment was liable to be arrested under "vagrancy" laws and put to hard labor in prison; white men and women, of course, were allowed to be unemployed.

Racial segregation increased in the following decades as Jim Crow laws required separation of the races in many public spaces. ("Jim Crow" was a derogatory name for blacks that had been in use since the 1830s.) Some black men were elected to Congress and state offices in the years immediately after the Civil War, but soon black men's hard-won voting rights were rescinded by these restrictive laws and mob violence. State laws sought to keep blacks subordinated to whites, and lynch mobs tortured and killed black men who stepped out of their allotted roles. Almost a century later, a new generation of activists would have to fight for the political, economic, and civil rights that Child had hoped would come with emancipation.

7

TWILIGHT YEARS

When Lydia Maria Child was about 70, David begged her to have a photograph taken just for him. Child described their conversation to the sculptor Anne Whitney: "I fell in love with your *honest shoulders*," David told her, "and I want you to have a photograph taken, on purpose for *me,* with the shoulders uncovered." Child was bemused by the "lover-like whim," but decided to give in to his pleas. "Having no low dress," she concluded, "I folded a shawl about the bust." All photographs at that time had to be taken by professional photographers, because cameras were too expensive for home use. We can only imagine what the photographer thought when a 70-year-old woman presented herself wrapped only in a shawl—but both Child and David were pleased with the results. Despite all of David's failings as a husband, and all the years that he and Child lived apart, their marriage never finally lost its charm.

Although her relationship with David became a source of peace and happiness, in other ways the 1870s were very difficult for Child. After promising the freed blacks that their future would be better, she watched helplessly as racist laws and social practices, backed by white violence and

Child was not sure she liked the photo on which this engraving was based. It showed her, she wrote to a friend, "wearing the somewhat defiant look of a 'strong-minded woman,' and a reformer." She preferred the photo on the cover of this book, which she thought made her look "positively handsome and lady-like."

unsympathetic courts, steadily reduced their freedoms. In 1874 the Republicans lost control of Congress and the idea of racial equality was declared dead.

Child was frequently asked to write for the *National Anit–Slavery Standard,* whose focus had shifted from calling for freedom for the slaves to advocating racial justice, and the *Woman's Journal,* the largest woman suffrage and women's rights paper. She often felt, however, that she was an old woman writing for a different age. The *Standard* folded in 1872 because it no longer had enough readers willing to support its message of racial equality. Most of the readers of the *Woman's Journal* were 30 or even 50 years younger than Child, and they often found her concerns quaintly old-fashioned.

The steady loss of Child's old friends underlined her sense that her world was coming to an end. Every year brought new deaths. Child still lived in sleepy Wayland, from which even a trip into Boston was an excursion, so she often lost friends whom she had not seen for months or years. When she made plans to visit Louisa Loring, one of her closest friends, David became sick and Child postponed the trip to take care of him. By the time she made it to the Lorings' home, Louisa was "alarmingly ill" and Child had time only to say good-bye before she died. Child was especially pained by Charles Sumner's death in 1874, which she associated with the passing of the antiracist ideals he had long fought for in the Senate.

No friend's death, however, could be as hard as David's. He had been sick for years, with bouts of diarrhea and "screaming rheumatism" in his joints that made it impossible for him to dress himself or do anything else. As she had with her father, Child stayed by his side during the bad times, nursing him and helping him as best as she could. He pulled through so many crises that neither of them recognized that his last illness was different from the rest until two hours before he died. Finally, according to Child, he fell asleep "as gently as a tired babe, with his head leaning on my shoulder."

With David gone, Child felt desolate. "We had such pleasant companionship intellectually," she wrote to her friend Susan Lesley, "and he was always kind and lover-like, up to the last day of his life. The tearing up of roots so deeply bedded, makes the heart bleed." The last 20 years of companionship had, it seemed, almost erased the memory of the difficult years

At age 75, David Child still had many of the qualities that had drawn Maria to him more than 40 years earlier. She always admired David's persistence, though she sometimes thought it misplaced, and she could not have been happy with a husband who did not have his degree of moral fervor.

when David was rarely home and rarely wrote. In retrospect, Child saw—or at least wanted to see—her marriage as a good one.

Child spent the six weeks after David's death sorting through their belongings, giving gifts to friends and libraries, collecting documents for antislavery archives, and disposing of David's other books and papers. Then she closed up the Wayland house and went to stay with a series of friends. Ironically, after all those years of longing for Boston culture, for art and music and literature, she found that she could no longer enjoy it. Sarah and Francis Shaw, with whom she spent the winter, lived in a beautiful mansion filled with artworks and maintained by numerous servants. Child appreciated their kindness, but she missed her little Wayland house and the simple satisfactions of doing her own housework. Early in the spring she returned to Wayland and her garden.

For the rest of her life Child would spend winters in Boston and the rest of the year in Wayland. Neither world satisfied her. Boston seemed artificial and her friends' homes were too luxurious for the "frugal housewife." Wayland was isolated and its earthbound farmers could not understand the aesthetic pleasures and political causes that Child still cared about.

Nevertheless, Child's last years had moments of happiness. Gifts and bequests from friends, combined with her book royalties, gave her a financial security she had never before experienced. As chopping wood and drawing water and even cooking meals became more difficult, she was able to pay for some domestic help. Much of her money, however, she gave to various groups that helped freed people gain education and economic independence. She enjoyed her increased ability to give money where she thought it would do good.

Like many other people confronting death, Child discovered a renewed interest in religion. She read widely in

Buddhist texts that had been translated since she wrote her *Progress of Religious Ideas* 20 years earlier, and she reread the Bible with a new intensity. She decided to make an "Eclectic Bible" of her own—a collection of "the best portions" of the world's many religions.

Aspirations of the World: A Chain of Opals would be her last book. It included selections from Greek, Roman, Buddhist, Jewish, Christian, Chinese, Persian, and Hindu writings, including many modern authors. Child arranged her selections in chronological order within general topics such as "Moral Courage," "Benevolence," or "Ideas of the Supreme Being." Opals, she explained in the introduction, reflect different colors in different lights, so they are a fitting symbol of people's changing perceptions of truth. Child was especially careful to identify Confucius, Lao-tzu, and Mencius as Chinese writers. Anti-Chinese sentiments were increasing and would soon produce the Chinese Exclusion Acts of 1882, which prohibited Chinese immigration to the United States. Child felt too old and tired to take on a new crusade, but she wanted to do her part to counter anti-Asian racism. All ages and nations, she insisted, have had "holy aspirations," and the "Eclectic Church" of the future would appreciate all of them without placing any one people or tradition above the others.

One more loss lay in store for Child. Shortly after William Lloyd Garrison visited her for a "long cozy chat," he became sick and died. Child's tribute to him appeared in the *Atlantic Monthly*—her last published writing. "In the very city," she noted, "where he had been dragged to prison to save his life from a mob, and where his effigy had been hung on a gallows before his own door, the flags were placed at half-mast to announce his decease." The abolitionists, so long denounced, were now honored for their courage and vision. This remarkable transformation of public opinion, Child concluded, proved that ideals of justice and humanity would ultimately triumph over all obstacles.

By this point Child rarely ventured out to visit anyone, but one afternoon the writer Elizabeth Stuart Phelps went to visit her. Much later, in her memoirs, Phelps described the cheap Boston boardinghouse where Child spent her last few winters as "dreariness personified": the neighborhood was isolated and unfashionable, the building old and run-down. Even the steep stairs to Child's room, Phelps reflected, suggested her thoughtful use of money. "Each one of them meant some generous check which Mrs. Child had drawn for the benefit of something or somebody, choosing this restricted life as the price of her beneficence." When the sun came out, however, Child revealed one of her few self-indulgences. She hung a prism in the window to catch the light, and she and her guests watched the beautiful rainbow colors reflect off the walls and the room's spare furnishings.

Later residents stand in front of Child's home in Wayland, Massachusetts. Much of the house had been rebuilt in 1863, after a fire swept through the house.

Child hoped that she would die in Wayland, and she got her wish. On October 20, 1880, she died of a heart attack. Her funeral was small, attended by a few remaining abolitionist friends, neighbors, nieces, and "poor people who had been recipients of her charity." As the service drew to a close, a magnificent rainbow filled the sky. Like an expensive opal—and Child's simple prism—the rainbow glowed with the beauty of diversity within unity. It was a fitting tribute to her life.

Child had the great satisfaction of seeing her dream of abolition—which almost everyone had said was impossible—come true in her lifetime. Her success was not complete; racism continued, perhaps even increased, and more than a hundred years later American society would still be deeply divided by race. Nevertheless, there would never again be slaves on American soil. Child helped accomplish this enormous goal in a time when women could not vote. She protested against her fetters—especially her lack of political rights—but she did not let these restrictions prevent her from seeking justice for others.

Although Child's literary career never recovered from her early embrace of abolitionism, she accumulated a remarkable number of "firsts." She was the first person to edit a successful children's magazine. She was the first person to write a domestic manual for people of modest income. She was the first person to publish a systematic study of slavery. She was the first person to write a "city" column about urban life. She was one of the first people to write an American historical novel, a history of women, and a book specifically designed for elderly people. Clearly she was an innovative as well as prolific writer. She managed to support herself and—much of the time—her husband with her pen.

Child was not, however, superhuman. She was subject to depression and despair, and at times she could be outright cranky. Some years she felt as if she had accomplished nothing with her life. Her marriage was often troubled, and she always regretted that she had no children. Two things, however, distinguished her from the many people of her time who are now forgotten. First, she had an inexhaustible faith that liberty and justice are worth fighting for and that they will ultimately prevail. Second, she continuously acted on that faith, in large ways and small, even when she did not know whether her actions would succeed. She did not—like her husband—embrace every enthusiasm that came along, but she did her best within each situation and repeatedly risked failure. After each setback, each disappointment, she nursed her wounds and then tried again.

CHRONOLOGY

February 11, 1802
Lydia Francis is born in Medford, Massachusetts

Summer 1815
Moves to Norridgewock, Maine

Summer 1821
Moves to Watertown, Massachusetts, and changes her name to Lydia Maria Francis

July 1824
Publishes *Hobomok*

September 1826
Starts to edit the *Juvenile Miscellany,* which will continue publication until July 1834

October 19, 1828
Marries David Lee Child

November 12, 1829
Publishes *The Frugal Housewife*

August 5, 1833
Publishes *An Appeal in Favor of That Class of Americans Called Africans*

May 1841
Moves to New York to edit the *American Anti-Slavery Standard,* which would become the *National Anti-Slavery Standard*

February 1843
Separates her finances from her husband's

May 1843
Resigns from the *National Anti-Slavery Standard*

August 1843
Publishes *Letters from New-York*

June 1850
Moves back to Massachusetts with David Lee Child

1856
Violence erupts in Kansas between pro-slavery and antislavery settlers

May 22, 1856
Preston Brooks canes Charles Sumner in the U.S. Senate chamber

October 16–18, 1859
John Brown and his men raid Harpers Ferry, Virginia

April 12, 1861
The Civil War begins when Confederate troops attack Fort Sumter

January 1, 1863
Abraham Lincoln issues the Emancipation Proclamation, which frees all slaves in the Confederate states but not in states loyal to the Union

April 9, 1865
The Civil War ends

November 1865
Publishes *The Freedmen's Book*

October 20, 1880
Dies in Wayland, Massachusetts

Further Reading

Books about Lydia Maria Child

Baer, Helene G. *The Heart Is Like Heaven: The Life of Lydia Maria Child*. Philadelphia: University of Pennsylvania Press, 1964.

Clifford, Deborah Pickman. *Crusader for Freedom: A Life of Lydia Maria Child*. Boston: Beacon Press, 1992.

Karcher, Carolyn. *The First Woman in the Republic: A Cultural Biography of Lydia Maria Child*. Durham: Duke University Press, 1994.

Karcher, Carolyn, ed. *A Lydia Maria Child Reader*. Durham: Duke University Press, 1997.

Meltzer, Milton. *Tongue of Flame: The Life of Lydia Maria Child*. New York: Crowell, 1965.

Meltzer, Milton, Patricia G. Holland, and Francine Krasno, eds. *Lydia Maria Child: Selected Letters, 1817–1880*. Amherst: University of Massachusetts Press, 1982.

Mills, Bruce. *Cultural Reformations: Lydia Maria Child and the Literature of Reform*. Athens: University of Georgia Press, 1994.

Osborne, William S. *Lydia Maria Child*. Boston: Twayne, 1980.

Stux, Erica, and Mary O'Keefe Young (illustrator), *Writing for Freedom: A Story About Lydia Maria Child*. Minneapolis: Carolrhoda, 2001.

20th-Century Editions of Selected Works by Lydia Maria Child

The American Frugal Housewife. 1829. Reprint: Mineola, N.Y.: Dover, 1999.

An Appeal in Favor of That Class of Americans Called Africans. 1833. Reprint, edited by Carolyn Karcher, Amherst: University of Massachusetts Press, 1996.

The Freedmen's Book. 1865. Reprint: New York: AMS Press, 1980.

Hobomok and Other Writings on Indians by Lydia Maria Child. 1824. Reprint, edited by Carolyn Karcher, New Brunswick, N.J.: Rutgers University Press, 1986.

Jacobs, Harriet A. *Incidents in the Life of a Slave Girl*. 1861. Reprint: Mineola, N.Y.: Dover, 2001. (Originally edited by Lydia Maria Child.)

Letters From New-York. 1843. Reprint, edited by Bruce Mills, Athens: University of Georgia Press, 1998.

The Mother's Book. 1844. 2nd ed. Reprint: Bedford, Mass.: Applewood Books, 1992.

Over the River and Through the Wood. Illustrated by Christopher Manson. Reprint: New York: North-South Books, 1993. (There are also several other editions with different illustrators and publishers.)

The Rebels: Or Boston Before the Revolution. 1850. Reprint: New York: AMS Press, 1978.

The Right Way the Safe Way, Proved by Emancipation in the British West Indies and Elsewhere. 1860. Reprint: New York: Arno Press, 1969.

Biographies of Child's Friends and Colleagues

Bartlett, Irving H. *Wendell and Ann Phillips: The Community of Reform, 1840–1880*. New York: Norton, 1979.

Byrant, Jennifer Fisher. *Lucretia Mott: A Guiding Light*. Grand Rapids, Mich.: Eerdmans, 1996.

Cox, Clinton, *Fiery Vision: The Life and Death of John Brown*. New York: Scholastic, 1997.

Gates, Henry L., ed. *Narrative of the Life of Frederick Douglass, an American Slave, Written By Himself*. New York: Laurel Leaf, 1997.

Hedrick, Joan D. *Harriet Beecher Stowe: A Life*. New York: Oxford University Press, 1994.

Kerr, Andrea. *Lucy Stone: Speaking Out for Equality*. New Brunswick, N.J.: Rutgers University Press, 1992.

Kornfeld, Eve. *Margaret Fuller: A Brief Biography with Documents*. Boston: Bedford Books, 1997.

Lerner, Gerda. *The Grimké Sisters from South Carolina: Pioneers for Woman's Rights and Abolition*. New York: Oxford University Press, 1998.

Mayer, Henry. *All on Fire: William Lloyd Garrison and the Abolition of Slavery*. New York: St. Martin's, 1998.

McFeeley, William S. *Frederick Douglass*. New York: Norton, 1995.

McKissack, Pat. *Sojourner Truth: Ain't I a Woman?* New York: Scholastic, 1992.

Painter, Nell Irvin. *Sojourner Truth: A Life, A Symbol*. New York: Norton, 1996.

Simon, Paul. *Freedom's Champion: Elijah Lovejoy*. Carbondale: Southern Illinois University Press, 1994.

Sterling, Dorothy. *Ahead of Her Time: Abby Kelley and the Politics of Anti-Slavery*. New York: Norton, 1994.

Taylor, Clare. *Women of the Anti-Slavery Movement: The Weston Sisters*. New York: St. Martin's, 1995.

Yates, Elizabeth, Nora S. Unwin, and Gary Lippincott. *Prudence Crandall: Woman of Courage*. Honesdale, Pa.: Boyds Mills Press, 1996.

BOOKS ABOUT THE SOCIAL AND POLITICAL ISSUES OF CHILD'S ERA

Conrad, Susan Phinney. *Perish the Thought: Intellectual Women in Romantic America, 1830–1860*. New York: Oxford University Press, 1976.

Dixon, Chris. *Perfecting the Family: Antislavery Marriages in Nineteenth-Century America*. Amherst: University of Massachusetts Press, 1997.

DuBois, Ellen Carol. *Woman Suffrage and Women's Rights*. New York: New York University Press, 1998.

Finkelman, Paul, ed. *His Soul Goes Marching On: Responses to John Brown and the Harpers Ferry Raid*. Charlottesville: University Press of Virginia, 1995.

Foner, Eric. *Reconstruction: America's Unfinished Revolution.* New York: Harper & Row, 1988.

Hawkins, Hugh, ed. *The Abolitionists: Means, Ends, and Motivations.* 3rd ed. Lexington, Mass.: Heath, 1995.

Henkin, David. *City Reading: Written Words and Public Spaces in Antebellum New York.* New York: Columbia University Press, 1999.

Kraditor, Aileen S. *Means and Ends in American Abolitionism: Garrison and His Critics on Strategy and Tactics, 1834–1950.* New York: Pantheon, 1969.

Macleod, Anne Scott. *A Moral Tale: Children's Fiction and American Culture, 1820–1860.* Hamden, Conn.: Archon, 1975.

Marks, Paula Mitchell. *In a Barren Land: American Indian Dispossession and Survival.* New York: William Morrow, 1998.

Ripley, C. Peter, Roy E. Finkenbine, Michael F. Hembree, and Donald Yacovone, eds. *Witness for Freedom: African American Voices on Race, Slavery, and Emancipation.* Chapel Hill: University of North Carolina Press, 1993.

Spann, Edward K. *The New Metropolis: New York City, 1840–1857.* New York: Columbia University Press, 1981.

Wallace, Anthony F. C. *The Long Bitter Trail: Andrew Jackson and the Indians.* New York: Hill & Wang, 1993.

Yee, Shirley J. *Black Women Abolitionists: A Study in Activism, 1828–1860.* Knoxville: University of Tennessee Press, 1992.

Yellin, Jean Fagan. *Women and Sisters: The Antislavery Feminists in American Culture.* New Haven: Yale University Press, 1989.

Musuems and Historic Sites

Medford Historical Society
10 Governors Avenue
Medford, MA 02155
Telephone: 781-391-8739

Contains a few items related to Child and many more related to life in the 19th century. Nearby, at the corner of Salem and Ashland streets, is the house where Child grew up. The Mystic Bakery, on Salem Street, occupies the lot where Child's father had a bakery and sold his "Medford crackers."

Norridgewock Historical Society
11 Mercer Road, P. O. Box 903
Norridgewock, ME 04957
Telephone: 207-634-5032 or 207-634-3231
www.tdstelme.net/~nhmuseum/

Exhibits do not contain anything that belonged to Child, but they give a flavor of what life was like in rural Maine when Child lived there as a teenager in her sister's home.

Wayland Historical Society
Grout Heard House
12 Cochituate Road
Wayland, MA 01778
Telephone: 508-358-7959

Has several items that belonged to Child, including letters, books she wrote and books she owned, a quilt she helped make, and a bonnet she wore for much of her life. A special Lydia Maria Child Tour focuses on artifacts and stories related to Child. Visitors can also see the outside of the nearby house in which Child lived on Old Sudbury Road, though it has greatly changed since 1880.

INDEX

Acknowledgments

Writing this book would have been much more difficult without Carolyn Karcher, whose work as a researcher and editor has helped restore Lydia Maria Child to her proper place in American history. I highly recommend Karcher's excellent biography, *The First Woman in the Republic: A Cultural Biography of Lydia Maria Child,* to anyone who wants a comprehensive, insightful, and beautifully written examination of Child's life and work.

I also wish to acknowledge the on-going love and support of my partner, Randy Smith, who eases my path in so many ways.

PICTURE CREDITS

TEXT CREDITS

p. 34: From *The American Frugal Housewife* (1829. Reprint. Mineola, NY: Dover Publications, 1999), 1–2, 16, 17, 86, 88

p. 44–45: From *An Appeal in Favor of That Class of Americans Called Africans* (1833. Reprint, edited by Carolyn Karcher, Amherst: University of Massachusetts Press, 1996), 27, 22, 28, 126–27, 141, 160, 186–187

p. 64–65: From *Letters From New-York* (New York: C. S. Francis, 1843), 95–6, 249–251; *Letters From New-York: Second Series* (New York: C. S. Francis, 1845), 281

p. 81: From *The Right Way the Safe Way, Proved by Emancipation in the British West Indies and Elsewhere* (1860. Reprint, New York: Arno Press, 1969), 86, 92

p. 100–101: From *The Freedmen's Book* (1865. Reprint. New York: AMS Press, 1980), 269, 274–76

Lori Kenschaft is an American cultural, intellectual, and gender historian, with a special interest in the history of social change and social thought. She has taught at Boston University and the Harvard Graduate School of Education, and is currently working on a history of Americans' attitudes towards taxation. She has a Ph.D. in American Studies from Boston University.

DATE DUE

#47-0108 Peel Off Pressure Sensitive